Tattoo

Rebecca D. Turner

Cover photography: Eric Luecker
Cover design: Stacy Luecker
Book design: www.essexgraphix.com
Arm provided by Ken Stone, Fort Worth, Texas
Editor: Tana Grubb (tanagrubb@hotmail.com)
Proofreader: Erin Hamilton (erin.hamilton@thomson.com)

Trafford Publishing
6E - 2333 Government Street
Victoria, BC, Canada V8T 4P4

www.readtattoo.com

ISBN: 1-4120-8456-3

Printed in the United States of America

TABLE OF CONTENTS

Introduction: The Agreement

"Nothing is more difficult, and therefore more precious, than to be able to decide."

— Napoleon Bonaparte
Considered one of the greatest military commanders
in our history (1750s to early 1800s)

"Most people are not afraid of dying: they are afraid of not having lived. What frightens them more is the dread of insignificance, the notion that we will be born and live and one day die and none of it will matter. What they desperately want is to live long enough to get it right, to feel that they have done something worthwhile with their lives."

— Harold S. Kushner
Living a Life that Matters

So who am I and how can I relate to you in your life and business so you can benefit from reading this book? Even though we are very different, if we can agree on a few small items, then reading this book will be worth your time.

The Agreement, a book by Dr. Thomas Michael Delagarza, states that anytime there are differences in a situation, the parties involved need to focus on points of agreement. I think that makes a lot of sense. Even though you and I are very different, if we can agree on a few small items, then you can benefit from reading this book.

You and I could be a different age, race, culture, religion, and we could even have a different belief about what is "right and wrong." You and I probably have a different education, and are possibly at a different socioeconomic place in our lives. You and I could get so caught up in how different we are that we become blind to seeing anything that we might have in common. Because we are all such unique individuals, with our own set of uniquely defined fingerprints and strands of DNA, what could we possibly have in common?

In fact when our firm counsels clients about what they want to do with their lives, we talk about what it is upon which we can agree. If we can agree on a few important facts as they relate to what they desire for their lives, then we can usually help them.

THE FIVE AGREEMENTS

1. Let's agree that you would like to increase the amount of business that you and your company generate.
2. Let's agree that you would like to spend less time working to generate more income, so you have more time to do what you love to do.
3. You agree that today at some level, partly because of technology, what you and I provide for our customers today are commodities. So after you have a decent product or service, the best, most cost effective way to increase business is through exemplary customer service. This is treating your customer better than they expect to be treated. This is done so much so that it creates an emotionally positive experience, resulting in a passionate customer, who is compelled to tell the story of their experience to others.
4. Let's also agree that if you can achieve both one and two and have more fun along the way doing it, you would want to do that.
5. And at the end of the day, you'd like to make a difference in this world.

After having stated these five points of agreement, are we all on the same page? Certainly all of us would like more money, more time, more fun in our lives and to end our lives knowing they weren't in vain, making a difference. If you can nod your head in agreement, then let's explore some ways to do just that.

In the next few chapters, I'm going to illustrate what a customer advocate is and just like the saying "you can never be too rich," why you can never have too many advocates. By having advocates for your business—people who go out and get business for you—you then have advocate marketing. Simply put: Passionate employees = passionate customer service = customer advocates = advocate marketing.

ADVOCATE MARKETING IMPOSTERS

This is more important today than ever as the conventional advertising methods don't work well anymore. Large corporations have figured this out and are implementing strategies today that are in effect what I call advocate-marketing imposters. These are either consumers or employees who are paid financially or compensated with products to go out and talk to others about how great a certain product is, and these imposters strongly encourage others to purchase the product for themselves.

You will learn why creating real advocates is not only more cost effective for you than conventional forms of advertising, but also easier to implement and more fun. We'll explore examples of three major corporations and how they have been implementing real customer advocates and advocate marketing (not imposters) for quite some time now, and are ahead of their competition as a result. There are also examples of small businesses, much like the one you might manage or own yourself, that create advocate marketing as well.

AS A CONSUMER & EMPLOYEE

Although the concepts in this book apply mainly to the business owner or manager who has the power to make changes in his or her organization, the concepts can be equally as applicable to employees and customers. After reading about how these companies, large and small, create wonderful experiences for both their employees and their customers, I think you will be enlightened as an employee or customer yourself. Just like the saying "a mind stretched to a new idea, will not be the same again," as an employee, you will choose to only work for companies who treat you well, and give you the empowerment like the companies described in this book. And as a consumer, you will be inspired to only do business with establishments that treat you as though you are worthy of their business. As a consumer you will realize that you deserve to be treated well by the companies that you patronize.

I have always wanted to write a book about "something." I say always because twenty years ago when I graduated from college my two college roommates and I sat down and played a little game. I asked each of us to say something that we wanted to accomplish in our lives before we die that we thought others would be surprised about. What I said was write a book. When my roommates inquired as to what I would write about, I told them, I didn't have a clue. Now twenty years later, because of many bad customer service experiences and some good ones, I feel I have something to "say" that is relevant and others could benefit from hearing.

One of my pet peeves is being treated unfairly or poorly by a company I patronize. It really gets under my skin to spend my hard earned money on a product or service and be treated as if I'm not valued by that company or treated in a manner that is unfair. When I am treated unfairly, I usually inquire to the employee, "If you were me, would you feel that you were being treated fairly?" When they break eye contact, look at the ground or state honestly that they agree with me, even though they might not have the power to change the situation, if nothing else, they agree that as the customer, I have been treated wrong.

So getting bad customer service is a pet peeve and that coupled with a story that a client shared with me last fall, it hit me, why not write a book about customer service? Now I admit the topic does sound a little boring but after seeing the title and cover of this book, I hope you "get" the fact that my goal is to make this topic exciting for you.

I first went to the bookstore and searched online for titles of books about customer service. I admit 90% of the titles were boring to me. But I bought and read the 10% of the books that didn't have boring titles. By the way, there weren't a lot to pick from that were just about customer service. Many books had chapters on customer service but not entire books on the topic. Again, advocate marketing comes from customer advocates that are inspired from passionate customer service given by passionate employees.

The stories I have to share in this book are all positive customer service stories. The only negative story I have to share is the story my client shared with me last fall and even though it is negative, I found it humorous.

THE TELLER AT THE BANK

The story goes like this. In order to open a specific account for a client who lived out of state, there was what is called a medallion signature guarantee required. We can handle this at our office in most cases, but since the client lived out of state, it was more convenient for them to go to a local bank to have this done.

They inquired at the bank to have this service done. They were told, "We're sorry, you have to be a customer of the bank for that service." My client asked, "I can't just pay you to have the signature guarantee done?" "No," the bank teller replied.

"So how do I become a customer of the bank?"

The teller, "You open a checking account."

"What is the minimum to open an account?"

"$100 dollars."

"So I could open an account for $100, and then close it and you could signature guarantee these forms."

"You have to keep the account open for 90 days or you will be charged a fee. And you aren't supposed to open an account with the intention of just closing it."

"How much is the fee to close an account prior to 90 days?"

"$30 dollars."

"Can't I just pay you $30 dollars, and we both save our time from my just opening and closing an account, so you will signature guarantee my form for me?"

To that the teller replied, "No, you have to be a customer of the bank."

Ok, does that not remind you of a mad version of "Who's on first?" Wouldn't it have made sense for the manager at this bank to charge, say $30 for this service for non-bank customers? The non-bank customer would have walked away having a good experience, and if they needed banking services in the future, because of this positive experience, they would consider this bank that helped them out with this one service. I seriously doubt that my client would consider this bank in the future.

I'm sure I wasn't the only one that heard about how inconvenient this particular bank is. As a result, this bank did not create an advocate for future business and possibly deterred future potential customers from even giving them a try. As a business owner and manager yourself, if you were the owner of this bank and you heard this story after it happened, I have to think that you, like me would have your skin crawling right now and are horrified of the bad image that your bank just created in possibly more than one mind of your potential customers.

Well, I hope you enjoyed that story and again it is the only negative customer service story in this book. After I got off of the phone, and the client had shared this story with me, a light bulb went off in my head, and I thought, "Write a book about good customer service."

I'd like to share how my experiences have prepared me to not only want to create the most positive customer experience possible for my clients, but also research companies who I have determined emulate the ten aspects of advocate marketing.

I am affiliated with the thirteenth largest company in the world of any kind, and we are a full service financial planning firm. As you can imagine, we have hundreds of services to offer our clients. Over the last seventeen years as I have observed and studied advisors inside and outside our firm, I have come to the conclusion that the best way to give our clients the attention they deserve is to work as a team among other advisors, who have the same philosophies and ethics that I do. We as a team also believe that the best way to give our clients the best advice for their unique situation is to have each of us specialize in a specific area.

I have been a financial advisor for seventeen years. Within our financial services firm, we are given the freedom to run our business like anyone self-employed. We can choose to hire and pay our own staff and have the freedom to treat our clients in the manner we choose, as long as we stay within the guidelines of the SEC, which allows us to keep our license to do business within our profession. Given the freedom that we do have in our business, there is no standard set for customer service. As long as no laws are broken that would cause us to loose our licenses, we can treat our customers or clients as good or bad as we want.

Since there is no policy on customer service, I felt the need to set a standard for my business partners and staff. Everyone on our team uses the customer service policy I developed. This policy provides a standard, which makes our client's "experience" with us above the average service they would expect. We want our clients to feel "taken care of," so they can be confident and at peace with where they are in their financial lives. Knowing that someone they trust is "taking care of them," then they can focus their precious time and energy on what they love in their life…their families, their businesses and their hobbies and special interests.

You will find many companies who are in the exact same business as you, and they no doubt do a decent job at the service they provide. So ask yourself, with so many "good" companies out there, what will set you apart from your competition? You will find it is the "little things," that make the difference in which company your customer chooses.

Furthermore, as you are reading this book, I think it will be hard

INTRODUCTION: THE AGREEMENT

for you not to think of your own customer service story—a story where you, the customer, were treated good or bad by a company. Today, the phrase "the customer is always right" often gets lost or changed to the "customer is wasting my time" or "why can't the customer look the information up on the website." The easier we make the experience of doing business with our customer, the more they will want to do business with us. If we provide not just a good experience but a "wow" experience, the more our customers will want to plead, beg and drag their friends and acquaintances to our door. The result you have produced is a customer advocate.

Through the remarkable and passionate customer experience you give your customer, you will be known in your industry for your customer service and create a story to be told by your advocates. Once you have created multiple customer advocates, you have produced advocate marketing. Having advocate marketing is cost effective, easy and personalized for your business.

INUNDATED WITH ADS AND PRODUCTS

As we are bombarded with more and more mass advertising, direct mail and spam, the more we will become immune to a company's plea for our dollar. In 1975, the average grocery store had 3,200 products on their shelves. Do you want to take a guess at how many there are today, on average? 64,000 yes that's right 64,000! As consumers, we have to sift through more products to find "the ones" we want. To save ourselves time, we have conditioned ourselves to ignore the advertising, displays etc. We focus only on what we are looking for. Additionally, our parents received 3,000 ads per year, and today you and I receive 5,000 ads per day!

Based on those unbelievable statistics, we are obviously going to have to get better and better at understanding our customer to reach them. We must focus on listening to what they want and delivering it to them in the manner they prefer, or we are going to become the needle in the haystack among our competition.

Companies like Starbucks, Ritz Carlton, and others like them have already figured this out and are household names with platinum reputations for the experiences they give their customers.

At the end of each chapter is a notes section for you to write down ideas that you can implement for your business. You can use this book as a workbook by writing about what you have learned after reading each chapter, then take what you have learned to improve your customer service and produce your own advocate marketing plan.

Whether you or your company become household names or not, it doesn't matter. You can become the go-to person or company for whatever product or service you provide, by creating an experience that your customers will want to come back to again and again and drag their friends with them. The result: your own advocate marketing plan.

Because over-the-top service in our fast paced "I don't have time for you society," is so desirable, that not only will they come back and bring their friends with them, but also they will pay a premium dollar for what you provide. Just ask Starbucks: $7.50 for a cup of Joe? No problem.

So again if you would like more money, more time and more fun in your life, as well as making a positive difference in other's lives, then we are in agreement. And now that we are in agreement, let's get started.

CHAPTER ONE

SO, WHAT'S WITH THE TITLE?

"It's not the destination it's the journey"
— **Tagline for Harley Davidson**
motorcycle company

"Life is either a daring adventure or nothing"
— **Amelia Earhart**
First woman of aviation and the first woman
to fly across the Atlantic Ocean (1920's)

Have you ever asked yourself "What would cause someone to voluntarily want to dye his or her skin with permanent ink displaying the logo of a brand name?" I probably don't have to give you too long to picture the Harley logo in your head. In fact, I'd be surprised, no matter where you live and what you do, if you haven't seen a Harley tattoo on someone, somewhere yourself.

I'd like to explore that kind of "I want to tattoo my body" passion as it relates to the Harley product, and how it relates to you and me in our businesses. We can learn a lot about this kind of passion. This passion is the essence for creating the advocate marketing that we need for our business to thrive in today's marketplace. One of the essentials is creating a positive customer experience so the consumer feels "compelled" to tell someone they know about the experience. This is at the heart of customer advocates and advocate marketing.

Let me begin by telling you a story about this product and the experience I had with Harley Davidson. I guess I have been a risk taker for most of my life. I have sky dived, rappelled and I think I have accepted most of the dares I was offered in my life, at least until I was 35. Then something happened. I started to become scared about everything. I had so many dreams that I wanted to accomplish, one of which was writing a book, and I couldn't picture my life north of 35 anyway.

To help you understand my mindset and personality, I'll share a story that happened a few years ago. I was a runner and at about this time in my life, my knees started swelling up after running, so I went to a knee specialist. After the doctor x-rayed my knees, he stated, "What on earth have you been doing, your knees look like they are 80 years old." To which I replied, "I didn't know if I'd make it this far, so hadn't thought much about saving myself for later."

I started doing something else at this wonderful age. Instead of requesting a window seat on flights so I could see everything, I started requesting an aisle seat so I couldn't see how high up we were, and so I could go to the bathroom without disturbing anyone. Ugh, getting older.

I had always wanted a Harley Davidson motorcycle. When I came to this point in my life, I thought that maybe if I got one, it would help me keep this part of myself, the risk taker, that I felt I was losing. So I was forcing myself to do something somewhat risky, but alas, ignoring the laughter of the other bikers I rode with, I always wore a helmet.

PHENOMENON

So as I dove into the Harley Davidson biking world, I discovered some very interesting things. If you're wondering what all of this has to do with customer service, it does.

The Harley phenomenon probably can't be 100% explained by any one criterion. And if you talk to a Harley motorcycle owner, they will likely tell you that if you don't own one, you won't "get" it.

If you haven't thought of the passion Harley owners have for their product by now, maybe after you give it some thought you will be curious, like I was, about what the passion is all about.

Being a former Harley owner, I can tell you a few interesting tidbits about the phenomenon behind the product. During the seven years that I owned two Harleys and rode in groups, some interesting things happened. I received more gifts than I ever have in my life, and from people I would least likely suspect would want to give me a gift.

As various people would give me a gift with the Harley logo, they all made about the same comment, "I saw this (t-shirt, coffee mug, photo frame etc.) and thought of you." I literally received more gifts during this period of my life, than I ever have. Many of these same people had known me for years, and I've certainly owned many other "products," but they never came to me with that same comment and handed me a t-shirt with a company's logo on it.

Why did this happen? I think for a few reasons. One reason is, just like having a single friend that others try to live vicariously through, many do this with Harley owners. There is a mystique about being carefree on an open road. Riding a Harley brings out the rebel that many of us wish we could be, or for some of us, be again.

Of course there is the aspect of independence and freedom associated with riding and of just being carefree and having fun. But for most people, even those who talk about owning a Harley someday, they never will. Something holds them back; a spouse that states it is too dangerous, or their own fear of possibly being hurt. Whatever the reason, most people will continue to buy Harley products for their Harley-riding friends, but never own one.

A LEGEND

Certain products become the envy of their peers; because of the reverence consumers have for that specific product by a company. It would be hard to argue against Harley Davidson, in the motorcycle world, not being the revered bike. In fact, many would call a Harley a legend.

I experienced this when I went to purchase a helmet before I actually bought my first bike. The non-Harley dealer that I went to for the helmet asked what I was planning on buying. I told him an 883 Sportster (the starter bike for most Harley riders). He then wanted to "show" me something that he thought might interest me. As he pointed out every feature on the bike, he would make the same comment, "And just like the Harley," this bike has or does this or that.

Now, my mind had been made up (actually when I was twelve years old, because I wanted to own a Harley, "someday") on buying a Harley. As he continued to show me features and repeat his favorite phrase, it occurred to me, why was he trying to get me to buy a product that resembled what I wanted, by continually comparing it to what I wanted, a Harley?

As I walked out of the store and thanked him for his time, I felt compelled to offer him a tip. I told him that in the future, "I wouldn't compare your brand of bike, to the bike someone really wanted as a way of selling them on your bike." It was as if the Harley, in this case was "the" bike to epitomize and everything else, including the bike he wanted me to buy, was somehow inferior.

So why did I choose to discuss Harley Davidson? Besides being curious about the phenomenon, I love the passion that Harley lovers have for their product. Most of the time, when someone has a passion for something, they will go to the nth degree to get you to understand why they are so passionate about it.

So forget about the product for a minute. What if you and I could instill just a hint of that I-want-to-tattoo-my-body-to-tell-everyone-my-passion, passion into our customers? Now we don't necessarily want our customers to tattoo their body, but surely we can learn something from their extreme emotion for this product. If we could capture some of that passion, our customers and clients would not only continue to buy from us, but like anyone who has ever known a Harley owner, they will get—or at least try to get—their friends interested in what we have to offer as well. This word-of-mouth advertising can create extreme success for small businesses as well as large. Customers and clients who become unofficial advocates or spokespersons can create quite a buzz for businesses that truly benefits the bottom line.

The sound of a loud Harley riding through your neighborhood on a quiet Saturday morning may make you annoyed. You may not even like motorcycles at all. Whether that is the case or not, I want to share with you some aspects about the company that you might find interesting. Try and have an open mind while you read about the passion of the employees and the success the company has had over the last several decades.

A SUCCESSFUL COMPANY

Harley Davidson, Inc. the parent of Harley-Davidson Motor Company (HDMC), has:

- Outpaced its own record performance in each of the last 18 years.
- Had 11 consecutive years of increased dividends paid to investors.
- 761 million of net income (up 31% from '02)
- 4.6 billion in total revenue (up 13% from '02)
- 650 million free cash flow (up 59% from '02)
- Return on average equity >20%
- 291,000 Harley Davidson units shipped (up 10% from '02)
- 36% gross profit margin (up from 34.7% in '02)

Additionally, Harley Davidson is considered the only major U.S.-based motorcycle manufacturer.

I offer these facts to establish in your mind that this is a successful company with a successful line of products and to explore with you some solid reasons why they are successful and how you can learn from them.

Think of your own business and how you might be able to capture some ideas from what they do to make your employees more passionate or make your business more successful.

THE EXPERIENCE

Let's start with Harley's mission statement, which pretty well spells out what they are trying to achieve with their clientele. "We fulfill dreams through the experiences of motorcycling. By providing to motorcyclists and to the general public an expanding line of motorcycles and branded products and services in selected market segments."

Harley further states, "It takes more than just building and selling motorcycles to fulfill the dreams of our customers. It takes unforgettable experiences. If there's one secret to our enduring brand and the passion it ignites in our riders, it's that we deliver these experiences, rather than merely a collection of products and services."

To make the dream of owning a Harley even more of a reality, in 1993 the company formed Harley-Davidson Financial Services. This added service to its customers offers a variety of financing and insurance options. This service can save the customer time and increase their ability to not only pick out a bike on a given day, but be able to leave, riding it home from the dealership.

CUSTOMIZATION

Appealing to the consumer's increasing desire to create specialization, Harley provides over a thousand accessories for its clientele to customize their own individuality into their bike. Riders have their own ideas about what makes a Harley special to them, and why it would be rare for you to ever see two Harley's designed alike.

PHILANTHROPY

Harley Davidson the company is also very philanthropic and encourages its employees to get involved in the betterment of the community. Harley has the "Strong Foundation," which focuses most of its resources on improving education and neighborhood revitalization.

The company also has an employee program called "dollars for hours," this program provides matching dollars to the employee's volunteer hours to the non-profit of their choice. Harley has also been a corporate sponsor of the Muscular Dystrophy Association. Over the course of two decades, they with their partners have raised over 40 million dollars towards fighting this disease.

MEMBERSHIP AND ITS BENEFITS

To insure and back up their desire to provide an unforgettable "experience" for its customers, in 1983 Harley introduced H.O.G. (Harley Owners Group). H.O.G. has more than 600,000 members worldwide. These groups offer members a wide array of events, rides and member benefits to get riders involved in riding, to increase the enjoyment of their experience of riding.

In addition, the 1,300 Harley-Davidson dealerships in 48 countries worldwide are not only a place to buy a bike and merchandise, but a place for riders to talk and meet their friends. Some dealerships have a restaurant and bar to create an atmosphere that says, stay awhile and enjoy the company of your Harley family. Dealerships are also known for weekend parties to celebrate all kinds of occasions. Hot dog stands, music, and games provide an atmosphere of fun for the entire family.

EMPLOYEES — THE ENGINE OF PERFORMANCE

The core values Harley uses for the decisions and contributions their employees make for the company is: Tell the truth, be fair, keep your promises, respect the individual, and encourage intellectual curiosity. Harley states, "We believe that our business will be most successful if we tap the contributions of each of our people."

Harley goes on to state that they believe the future growth and viability of the company depends on their ability to value both differences and similarities among their employees. Harley's belief in their words, "we would not be where we are today without the passion of all of those who work for our company and their desire to make a difference in our business." In fact, Harley comments that "employees are the engine of our performance and the foundation of the company's success."

EMPLOYEES, "GREATEST COMPETITIVE ADVANTAGE"

As you look further into what makes the company tick, you will find a passion in the employees that is prevalent and unique to corporate America. In fact Harley emphasizes that they "consider our employees to be our greatest competitive advantage." One way they instill employee involvement is that layers of management are kept at a minimum and an "open door" policy extends throughout the company.

Harley believes that easy access to senior management backs up their desire to believe in employees. In the late 1980s Harley created the Harley-Davidson Business Process. The idea behind the process is for the company to share its vision, so that employees will work as a group, with their efforts working in the same direction.

EMPLOYEE INVOLVEMENT

To make this idea a reality, Harley encourages salaried and unionized workers to participate in key business decisions. There are two unions represented in the Harley organization, the International Association of Machinists (IAM) and the Paper Chemical Workers (PACE) union.

To continue the company's innovation in involving employees at all levels, in 1995, Harley formed a unique partnership relationship with the unionized workforce. Through partnering, Harley believes the company can benefit from the thinking of all of the employees. Harley also recognizes employee involvement as an enabler of success.

At Harley, operations are grouped into three broad areas:
1. **The Create Demand Circle:** marketing and sales functions for

motorcycles, parts and accessories, new business development, customer service, motorcycle styling, government affairs, and owners groups.

2. **The Produce Products Circle:** the engineering function, manufacturing operations, materials and cost management, and quality functions.

3. **The Provide Support Circle:** includes finance, human resources, legal, information services, communications and strategic planning.

Circle leaders jointly manage their respective circle business and develop strategy. No single person is the circle leader. Instead, the leader role of each circle changes to different individuals based on the issue being addressed.

All three circles overlap to form the Leadership and Strategy Council (LSC). The LSC is comprised of members from each circle, along with the Chief operating officer of Harley-Davidson Motor Company, Buell (Buell is Harley's sport performance bike) Motorcycle Company and Harley-Davidson Financial Services, and the CEO of Harley-Davidson Inc. This collaborative effort is responsible for making decisions on business issues impacting the entire company, developing high-level policies and consulting with the Chief Executive Officer.

To further back up their words with actions, Harley has a bonus plan that is tied to the company's performance.

EMPLOYEE PASSION

The passion for the product is not just for customers. According to the company, an estimated 80% of employees are Harley owners. Another interesting tidbit Harley uses to engage the employee and make them feel a part of the company: the people you see in those Harley merchandise magazines—high paid models? Nope. Harley employees.

Let's review how **Harley** accomplishes each of the ten attributes of advocate marketing:

- **Differentiating factor:** the Harley mystique, the rebellious attitude, experience and freedom associated with Harley. The product being more of a "legend."
- **Customer loyalty:** "600,000 H.O.G. members worldwide." "80% of employees are Harley owners."
- **Saving the Customer time:** Harley Financial Services, "you can pick out your bike, meet with the finance person and ride home in the same day."
- **Customer "experience" so a "story" is told about the company:** Part of the Harley mission statement is: "We fulfill dreams through the experiences of motorcycling." "It takes more than building and selling motorcycles to fulfill the dreams of our customers. It takes unforgettable experiences." "One secret of our enduring brand and the passion it ignites in our riders is that we deliver these experiences, rather than merely a collection of products and services." To insure and back up their desire to provide an unforgettable experience for their riders, in 1983 Harley formed H.O.G. (Harley Owners Group).

  "In addition, 1,300 dealerships in 48 countries worldwide are not only a place to buy a bike and merchandise, but a place for riders to talk and meet their friends. Some dealerships have a restaurant and bar to create an atmosphere that says stay awhile and enjoy the company of your Harley family. Dealerships are known for weekend parties to celebrate all kinds of occasions. Hot dog stands, music and games provide an atmosphere for the entire family."
- **Create customization in your product or service:** "over 1,000 accessories to add on to your bike." "It would be hard to ever see two bikes designed alike."
- **Employees feel apart of the company:** Provide benefits that make employees feel valued and a part of your company. Let them know your percentage increase in profits and provide a bonus plan based on those percentage increases if possible.

Create a positive employee "experience," so they feel a part of your company and feel they receive the maximum benefit from what you have to provide them. Using employees in Harley merchandise magazines as models certainly makes employees feel apart of the company.

- **The forgiveness factor:** When Harley was bought by AMF, in 1969, the quality of the product declined considerably. In fact, motorcyclists would joke about a Harley spending more time in the shop for repairs than on the road. In 1981, thirteen Harley Davidson's senior executives purchased the company from AMF. It took awhile for consumer confidence to believe in the product again, but since the company's IPO in 1987, Harley has seen double-digit growth every year. In a sense, all was forgiven, and the Harley consumer was glad to have the product that had built its reputation, back in the marketplace.

- **Is the customer willing to pay a premium?** For the same cc motor, and comparable accessories, the bike's cost is on average 18% more than a comparable bike sold by a competitor. (Based on the 2005 price of a Harley 883 Sportster and a 2005 Honda 750 Shadow Spirit).

- **Does the competition try to emulate the product?** American Iron Horse, Big Dog motorcycles and companies like them produce high end motorcycles comparable to Harley Davidson bikes. Those companies and companies like Honda that produce bikes like the Shadow and Vulkair, have all come to the market after Harley's success. And their product's emulate features of a Harley body style and accessories. It would be hard to argue that the popularity of TV shows like American Chopper can not partially attribute their success to the groundwork Harley laid for them with the increasing success they have had over the last two decades.

 The most telling comments in regard to this attribute: I have not heard of another motorcycle being given the status of a "legend."

- **Don't think big, think small:** The concept of using Harley employees in their merchandise magazines I find very interesting.

We all want our own five minutes of fame, don't we? What better way to engage their employees by giving them the opportunity to pose wearing Harley gear and be "featured" in their merchandise catalogs?

It is similar to when I found Ken Stone (the man who belongs to the arm on the cover of this book) to have photographed. A friend asked me if I had to pay him. Pay him? His only question was, "When does the book come out, and do I get a copy?

Let's face it, if someone offered you the opportunity to pose for free in a magazine of the company you are involved with, you'd do it wouldn't you?

Notes:

_____

_____

_____

_____

_____

_____

_____

_____

_____

_____

_____

_____

_____

_____

_____

_____

_____

_____

WHY CUSTOMER ADVOCATES?
WHY ADVOCATE MARKETING?

"A good man is a man who isn't worried about his own career but rather the career of those who work for him."
— **Norman Augustine**
Author and former CEO
of Martin Marietta (1970-1990's)

"At every crossing on the road that leads to the future, each progressive spirit is opposed by a thousand appointed to guard the past."
— **Maurice Maeterlinck**
Belgium author and speaker who received
the Nobel Prize in 1911 for literature

Did you know research reveals that customers tell an average of twenty people about moments of misery but they only tell ten people about the wonderful moments they have with us? So we must create twice as many good experiences as bad ones just to break even!

But what if we change the experience somehow so that it is so memorable, that it leaves a lasting impression on our customers so they feel passionately compelled to tell others about it?

LOYAL CUSTOMERS VERSUS CUSTOMER ADVOCATES

Generally, customers continue to be faithful to your establishment as long as they continue to get their packages on time or you don't burn a hole in their clothes. But why stop with loyalty when you can create passion in your customer as the result of the awe inspiring experience they had with you? And the result: an advocate for your business.

Webster defines **loyal** as faithful to a cause, ideal or custom.

Contrast the definition of the word loyal to the definition of the word advocate.

Advocate — To plead in favor of

Plead — To entreat or appeal earnestly

THE CUSTOMER EXPERIENCE

You can create your own personal marketing representatives, one by one. As each customer experiences what you have to offer, they are inspired and moved to action to bring you more advocates just like them. Does the picture I painted of the Harley owner pleading with his friends come to mind?

A customer becomes a loyal customer once you do something to cause them to want to repeatedly patronize your business. A customer advocate is someone who is loyal to you and your business, but is also more than that. Because they had such a good experience doing business with you, they want the favorite people in their world to "experience" it for themselves.

You can always spot an advocate because they will begin by telling you a "story" of their experience. There is a story to tell because there were strong positive emotions engaged in this person's experience.

Experience defined: the state or result of being engaged in an activity. The key word here is **engage**: to attract or hold by influence of power.

Wow, no wonder Harley Davidson spends so much time creating the delivery of the ultimate experience. In fact, their tag line, "It's not the destination, it's the journey" is really a way of stating it's not the destination, it's the experience. But Harley isn't alone. Starbucks Ritz Carlton, and local stores you patronize spend time creating an experience for customers. You just might not have thought of it that way until now. And doesn't creating an amazing experience for your customer sound like a great reason to be excited to go to your place of business everyday?

THE POWER OF STORY TELLING

In *Jesus Life Coach* business consultant Laurie Beth Jones discusses being hired by an organization in New York. This organization had just issued a round of layoffs, and the executives at the organization wanted her to help it and its employees move forward on a new initiative. When Laurie Beth asked, "Why did you hire me?" The executive replied, "Because you are a story teller, and we need you to tell us a new story about who we are." This leader saw the value in stories and how they relate and make an impression on our lives.

Scientists tell us that the mind remembers emotional events and facts far better than when no emotion is attached to an event. The emotion actually improves our memory and authors and speakers who discuss the ability to recall people's names talk about attaching "stories" around a person's name to help remember it.

A book that was recommended to our firm for effectiveness in consulting with our clients is *Storyselling* by Scott West and Mitch Anthony. It is a book about how to illustrate a point you are trying to make by telling a story about it.

In 2005, our firm hired a consulting firm, (ASGMC, Inc. Jan Sparrow and Scott Asalone www.asgmc.com) to help us work better together and create better service to our clients. Jan shared with us the outcome of a study done at Harvard that was alarming to me, but it also really made me think about what we do for people everyday. The study revealed that 90% of patients, when told their behavior was life threatening, chose not to change that behavior. In our business we encourage people to make positive changes to their financial lives so that they can meet their goals.

I wondered, when most people don't apparently change their behavior when it is life threatening, how can we help them make positive changes in their financial lives?

THREE THINGS THAT CAUSE CUSTOMERS TO CHANGE THEIR BEHAVIOR

The Harvard study found three things that would cause a positive change in a consumer's behavior. One, it was perceived by them to be "personalized or customized" for them. Two, it was presented in a "concise" manner. We have too much information today and no time to decipher it. And third, there was an "emotional hook" that made them inspired or uplifted. The consultant went on to say that people will choose to work with us and won't necessarily remember our name, but they will remember our "story."

You can probably think of a time that your experience with a company was so great that you wanted to tell the story of your experience over and over to whoever would listen. Maybe it is a particular storeowner who remembers your name every time you walk in his store.

Now after bragging about the store and telling your friends about it, you want them to experience it, too. You would have to have confidence that your friend's experience lived up to the stories you have told. You would have to know beyond reasonable doubt that this experience would happen for your friend as well. You would have this confidence because every time you had patronized the business, your experience was wonderful each and every time. You would not brag on and on about a company unless you knew your friend would be equally delighted once they walked through that business's door.

If all of the pleading and begging and reminding didn't entice your friend to go to the business on their own, as an advocate, you would offer to pick them up so you could go together.

PASSIONATE CUSTOMERS

Passion is intense emotion compelling action. A person's emotion is so strong that they can't help themselves from wanting to share or tell a story about what it is that causes them to be compelled to share it with whoever will listen. I see all different types of people in all different industries and positions within companies. When I meet someone who is passionate about something, I find it intoxicating.

In Harvey Mackey's book *How to Swim With the Sharks Without Being Eaten Alive,* he discusses how to get in front of the busiest people. The busier the person the more likely they are to be successful. They will also probably have a gatekeeper, the person who answers and screens calls to make sure only people of importance get through on the phone line.

Mackey discusses how, if you find out what this person is passionate about, you can inquire about their "passion," and he or she will likely talk in length to you. I've seen it happen often when a busy successful person sets an appointment and because they are busy, I mean who isn't today, they tell me "I only have 15 minutes." That same business owner or CEO will tell their assistant to hold their calls, or tell them to let their next appointment know that they will be 15 minutes late for their next meeting. Why? So they can finish their story about how they got started in business, or their grand child's first baseball game.

Passion; it's intoxicating.

By implementing a few small things into what you do and the service you provide each day, you can create passion that produces an advocate for your business. You and I can create customer advocates that we couldn't keep quiet, even if we wanted to.

"RING AROUND THE ROSY"

I'd like to share a story with you that relates to this kind of word-of-mouth advertising, the connectivity of people, and the contagious advocates that you and I create for our businesses. I only learned of this fact in 2000 when I went to England. I took a bus tour, and the tour escort was a historian who told some really amazing stories. One was the story of the game that children play called "Ring around the Rosy." If you are like me, you'll be surprised at its origin.

Authorities now agree that the bubonic plague or Black Death, killed one third of Europe's population between 1347 and 1350. This would mean that over twenty-five million people died of the disease. Obviously, this was a very dark part of Europe's history. Originally the words were "ring-a-ring o'roses" which referred to the red rash that people would get once they had the disease. "A pocket full of posies" referred to the superstition that if you put rose petals in your pocket, it would ward off the evil spirits associated with the plague. "A-tishoo! A-tishoo!" addressed the constant sneezing that was associated with those afflicted.

The next verse originally was "ashes to ashes," and has been changed over time to "ashes, ashes." This verse describes what was done to try and stop the disease from spreading: the bodies were burned. "We all fall down," the last line of the verse, alludes to what would most likely happen to those afflicted: death. It is recorded that people in their villages would gather frequently in the streets and dance hysterically in anticipation of "tomorrow we die."

At the time of the plague, people of all ages danced and sang together in large groups, until completely exhausted. It is believed that this frantic dancing relieved the anxiety that people felt during this difficult time. This dancing and singing continued long after the plague was over, but the adults no longer participated. Only the children continued singing the verse and dancing and eventually created a rhyme out of the original version.

The "song" as a nursery rhyme first appeared in Kate Greenaway's *Mother Goose*, in 1881. Isn't it interesting that 658 years later, we can walk by a playground and hear children singing this song? How did this happen? By word of mouth, by being passed down from children through the years, and by the contagious connectivity of people.

Twice since I started writing this book, I have been reminded of the song, "Ring around the Rosy." Last fall, 2004, I bought a Dave Matthews CD titled *Some Devil*. On the CD was a song called "Grave Digger" which includes the verses from this "nursery rhyme." The second time was when I took a friend's daughter to swimming lessons and what was one of the last games we played with the children? "Ring around the Rosy."

When you think that word-of-mouth advertising doesn't work, and it is not worth spending your time on, remember this "story."

So based on my research, life experiences and from hearing stories of good and bad customer service, I came up with a term that I call the most efficient, fun and cost effective way to grow your business—advocate marketing. And here are the ten simple, cost effective ways to create it through passionate customer service that will keep customers coming back for more.

The Ten Attributes of Advocate Marketing:
1. Differentiating factor: What is it that this company does that is different from the competition and is its distinguishing characteristic?
2. Does customer loyalty exist? Is the same product or service delivered consistently with the same positive results over time to build customer loyalty?
3. Has something been implemented to save the customer time?
4. Is the customer "experience" strong enough to create emotions in customers so they want to tell a "story" about it?
5. Has the product or service been customized or personalized for the customer or has something been implemented that makes the customer feel special?
6. Do employees feel a part of the company and its mission, enough so they carry out the customer experience, not because they have to but because they want to?
7. The forgiveness factor: If there is a mistake, will the customer give the business one, even more than one more chance?

31

8. Is the customer willing to pay a premium (more than the average price) for this product or service?
9. Has the competition tried to emulate a feature or benefit of the product or service because of the success the company has had or because the consumer has demanded it, due to the competition?
10. Don't think big, think small: What are the little things that are done that create an emotional hook for the customer, so they become passionate about your product or service?

Before we get into the other chapters that offer great examples of how businesses have used the attributes to enhance their success, we will explore them.

DIFFERENTIATING FACTOR

We have already addressed the fact that what we offer our customer today is a commodity. For most services, customers can go to a number of places to get what we have to offer. Not to mention the ease of ordering our "stuff" on the internet. We have to do something to differentiate us from our competition.

DOES CUSTOMER LOYALTY EXIST?

Do we deliver the same consistent product or service so well that our customers are for the most part repeat business for us? We have to be consistent so our customers continue to get what they have come to expect from our company.

I have a few Fort Worth small business stories that revolve around one establishment, Sewell Lexus, formerly Hillard Lexus. I have purchased several vehicles from this dealership over the last seven years. I continue to be amazed at their level of customer service.

One incident happened when I needed a new battery. Now, I realize that they probably looked at my buying history, and could tell I was about due to purchase another vehicle, but that didn't taint how special they made me feel on one of my visits.

After my battery was installed, I went to the check out window to pay for the service. The employee at the counter pushed the receipt for the battery and installation towards me, and thanked me for coming in. I stated that there must be a mistake as I received a new battery. She assured me pointing to my receipt that she was aware of the battery and installation, but that there was no charge for me today for this service.

As I walked out, I had to smile. They probably knew they had my loyalty based on my past patronage, they didn't know for sure if I was ready to buy a new car or not, but they wanted to make sure that if I did, I would continue my loyalty to their establishment.

And how much was their expense for that kind of marketing? The cost of whatever a battery is these days, and I suppose labor too.

But what are they getting in return besides my loyalty? Well, I did tell that story to numerous people, and now I am telling you and however many people choose to read this book. For whatever cost a battery and labor is these days, I would imagine that is pretty inexpensive advertising.

HAS SOMETHING BEEN IMPLEMENTED TO SAVE THE CUSTOMER TIME?

Our current society is fast-paced and continues to be more so than ever before. Time has become for many of us, our most valuable asset.

I live in Fort Worth, Texas. My home is only a few miles from my office downtown. I have lived in the same neighborhood for twelve years. For the last eleven years, I have changed dry cleaners randomly, depending on my mood that day or possibly based on a coupon offering a discount that I received in the mail. There are at least five different dry cleaners located conveniently on my way to work. Now I probably wouldn't go out of my way to try a dry cleaner, that wasn't convenient for me. Being conveniently located for me between home and work is definitely a criteria.

During the eleven years that I have used the five different locations, I never really noticed a difference in the quality of the dry cleaning service. They all did a "good" job. Because the quality was about the same at all five locations, I never developed a loyalty to any one in particular. That randomness ended a year ago.

One particular day, I piled the mound of clothes that had accumulated since my last trip to the cleaners into my car. Dropping off clothes to me is a hassle, and I often can't make the deadline to pick them up in the evening and don't always have time to drop them off on my way into work in the morning. In this particular mound of clothes, was a pair of slacks that was missing a button. I had conveniently forgotten about the missing button and the slacks were deep in the pile, when I dropped them off at a particular cleaners named, Twin Kell.

A few weeks later, as I was going through the cleaning that I had picked up, I noticed a long tag attached to a button on a pair of pants. I remember thinking that the tag resembled the note you receive in a fortune cookie. Both in the type set of the words on the tag and the width of the note itself. The tag read "your button has been replaced, compliments of Twin Kell." The missing button on the pair of pants that I had conveniently forgotten about, probably because I didn't want to take the time to do it myself, had been miraculously replaced by the button fairies at Twin Kell, at no charge.

I probably don't have to tell you but at that moment, for me, I knew that I wasn't going to be jumping around to different dry cleaners, anytime soon. But I did consider, maybe they don't "always" repair a button free of charge, and can they really catch the needed button "all" of the time?

So I did a test. I had a pair of slacks with an eye hook missing. I purposely threw them in the middle of my mound of clothes and didn't tell a soul. When I picked up this particular group of clothes, I couldn't wait to see the results of my test. I discovered the pair of pants with a familiar tag attached to a newly sewn eye hook replacement. The fairies at Twin Kell did it again. Not only did they find the problem they fixed it without my asking and again, no charge.

I still want to know how these employees have been trained to find clothes that need mending and what causes them to care enough to take the time to do it. That one small thing caused me to want to be loyal to Twin Kell because they saved me time by fixing the clothes that needed mending. Remember, in eleven years, I never noticed a difference in the quality of the different dry cleaners I frequented, or the timeliness of their service. They all did a "good" job.

On a separate incidence with Sewell Lexus, my lease was up in March of a particular year. I received a phone call in December from my sales representative, Mark Folchert. He wanted me to consider buying a car in December versus waiting until March to trade in my lease. I told him I didn't have time to drive out to the dealership, go through mounds of paperwork and switch cars. It was the end of the year, and we were busy finishing the business for the year. I let him know how crazy my life was during the last few weeks of December and was getting home at 8 p.m. every night, and I just didn't want to take any extra time right then to do it.

He then asked me a question, "So it's really your time that is the concern here, not whether you do or don't want to trade in your car?" I stated that he was correct, I was going to get the same car, in the same color, with the same options, and it didn't matter to me if it was now or in March. I'll never forget our conversation and what he went on to say. "If I fill out the application for you and bring it to your home, with the car, would you go ahead with the new lease today?" I hesitated. I appreciated his creativeness and willingness to meet me half way. This was really more for him, as again December or March, it made no difference to me. Also, I still had to take everything out of my car. Then I remembered, "What about setting my automatic garage door opener in the new car?" When he replied, "I'll take care of that for you when I bring you your car," I confess, he had me, and I gave in.

His willingness to work with me on my terms, and his ability to uncover my objection and then come up with a solution, made me want to do more business with him. This was another example of this establishment continuing to create loyalty in me, as their customer.

Because the representative made it so easy to do business with him, and he found a way for it to take virtually none of my time, he earned my business.

Is the customer "experience" strong enough to create emotions in customers, enough so they want to tell a "story" about it?
"Ring around the rosy," was a story told through a song that had obvious emotions attached to it. When emotions are attached to a persons name or to an event, research tells us that our memory is strengthened because emotions are involved.

The cleaners I mentioned earlier, Twin Kell, has another unique touch that they have implemented. When you pick up your clothes they hand you a scratch off card that has a treasure chest on it.

Remember the treasure chest when you were a kid that was at your doctor or dentist office? After being good on your visit you were allowed to help yourself to a piece of candy that was in the treasure chest. That is the kind of treasure chest on the scratch off coupon at Twin Kell. You scratch it off as you pick up your clothes, and you can win from 10%-40% off your dry cleaning for that visit. No coupons to cut out and remember to bring in, which saves one time from searching for them.

Now I don't think for a minute that this store marks up their dry cleaning by say 20%, so they can afford to give you these discounts. But let me ask you, after you receive the "fortune cookie" experience or the "experience of winning" by scratching off your discount, would you care if they did? I think that you, like me, know how busy we are, and how valuable our time is. And the experience of doing business with Twin Kell has proven to be one that stories are made of.

Another story that involves Sewell Lexus centers around the free car wash that the former owner Hillard had implemented every Saturday. When the new management took over they decided to discontinue the free Saturday car wash. Now I realize that most of these car owners could afford to pay for their own car wash. But every Saturday morning there they were lined up for their free car wash. No matter who we are or how much we make we all like the experience of being treated special. So when the new owners of the Lexus dealership decided not to continue the car wash, they weren't prepared for what happened.

The first Saturday after the buy out, there was a line of faithful Lexus customers lined up for their free Saturday car wash. This continued every Saturday for several months. And each Saturday a few of the customers would park their car, walk in and express their disappointment of Sewell not continuing the car wash. It took about three months for the managers and owners to discuss what they should do about the situation. The conclusion was to continue the car wash every Saturday, as it had been done by the previous ownership.

This truly was an experience that these customers valued. And besides, what do the customers do while they wait for their car to be washed? That's right they walk around and look at the new models on the lot. What better way to keep your loyal customer in front your product on a regular basis?

Has the product or service been customized or personalized for the customer or has something been implemented to make the customer feel special?
In today's fast-paced world most of us have within us the inherent desire to feel special. The busier we become as a society even to the point of not spending quality time with the special people in our lives, the more important it will become for us to have someone treat us as if we are special. Even if that "someone" is a large or small business who has figured out a way to do so.

Do employees feel a part of the company and its mission enough so they carry out the customer experience, not because they have to but because they want to?
I have always felt that from my own experiences with staff and from witnessing employees at businesses I encounter, the best employees

are the ones who act self-employed. If they act like they are owners, and have a vested interest in the business then they will treat the customer as the owner would.

From my experiences there are four factors to create staff that feels "ownership" in their employer's business.

- Reward employees monetarily and through recognition: The reward, whether recognition or monetary, needs to be with some kind of tie-in to the success or increase of business. Show the employee how recognition and reward levels are obtained so they are involved in the process and are a part of the experience.
- Empower employees to make their own decisions. This gives them confidence and, if empowered to tackle the small day-to-day decisions, they will be better prepared to handle the crisis that will occur when you or others in management are absent.
- Challenge your staff to put themselves in the customer's shoes: What if I were this customer, what would be a fair resolution?
- And lastly, hire the employees that have the mentality or desire to be self-employed, but who doesn't have the resources or confidence to actually start their own business.

THE GALLUP ORGANIZATION

The Gallup Organization, has coined the phrase "employee engagement." They use a 12 question test called the Q12 to determine how "engaged" an employee is in their company. When an employee feels disengaged at their company, they feel their opinion isn't important. This foresight is expressed by Marcus Buckingham, who worked for Gallup for 17 years, and now authored the book, *"The One Thing You Need to Know."*

The Gallup organization uses a dozen questions called the Q12 to predict what it has coined "employee engagement." Jim Harter, Gallup's Q12 chief scientist states that companies with disengaged executives can undermine a company. These executives are likely to have disengaged employees and create what Harter calls, "a cascading effect."

These disengaged employees will sometimes lash out with frustration from being treated like their opinions aren't important. While lashing out, these employees will steal, call in sick, and even bad mouth the company in revenge for how they have been treated.

So how we treat our employees can have a direct result on how our customers are treated. And it makes sense, doesn't it? I think by making your employees feel a part of your company (or as Gallup states, "engaged"), by allowing employees' input, you can avoid this costly mistake.

When you and I engage our employees, they feel their opinions count and state that their development is encouraged and they receive praise for their efforts.

I'm sure you aren't much different than us and our firm, when it comes to your staff's salaries and benefits. Your costs are rising. And you probably think the only way to keep great employees is by increasing their salary and benefits. But a study done in 2000 by the University of Dallas found that there was no correlation between CEO pay and engagement, or even CEO pay and company loyalty.

So apparently, even though I'm sure our staff appreciate the bonuses and raises we give them, what matters more once fair pay is received is to feel, like I have stated earlier, a part of the company.

Three of Gallup's 12 questions are key to creating "engaged" employees. The first question is: The mission/purpose of my company makes me feel my job is important. Secondly: At work, my opinions seem to count. And third: This last year, I have had opportunities to learn and grow.

When I read about the Gallup 12, I decided to ask my own staff those top three questions. I challenge you to do the same. And if one of your employees says no, do like I did and ask "What can we change or implement so you can answer yes to those three questions?"

One of the most interesting questions that received a higher score when an employee was engaged: "Do you have a friend that works at your company?" This tells me that the "social" aspect of our jobs is important to most of us. This makes sense when we spend 40-80 hours per week of our time at work, that enjoying the people we work with is important.

WHALE DONE

In Ken Blanchard's book, *Whale Done,* he discusses how whale trainers get a killer whale to do what they want them to do. As you can imagine, you don't force a killer whale to do anything. He actually applies the killer whale training methods to the management of people and how to get them to do what you want them to. He comments on the fact that once you and I implement new technology or a new way of servicing our clients that if it is good, it will be repeated by our competition. He goes on to state that, "the one thing your competition can never steal from you is the relationship you have with your people, and the relationship they have with your customers."

I think that quote sums up for us the direct impact our customers receive as a result of how we treat our staff.

You and I can create the "cascading effect" that the Q12 scientist, Harter, describes, but we can cause it to have a positive result by how our employees feel about our companies mission, and how they in turn, treat our customers.

The large corporations referenced in this book can throw all the marketing and advertising money they want at their customers, but without the company creating passion in employees, it will be hard to deliver the "experience" that the owner had in mind for his customer. The delivery of the "experience" is given by the employee. Much like the customer, making the employee feel engaged and a part of the company will make them want to deliver the wonderful experience even when you or management is not around.

THE FORGIVENESS FACTOR

If there is a mistake, will the customer give the business one, even more than one more chance? A Harvard study focused on doctors who were involved in lawsuits and doctors who for whatever reason, were not typically sued. Now I don't know, but if I was the one who requested the study, I'd guess that the doctors who did not become involved in lawsuits had more staff, or better trained staff. I might also guess that maybe they just hadn't been in practice as long or performed as many surgeries as the other doctors, who tended to be sued more often. Those would all make sense to me, and probably you as well.

But none of these were the answer. It actually had nothing to do with the number of staff or the skill of the doctor or the staff. The study found that doctors with less staff and experience were not necessarily sued more. Further, it found that, are you ready for this? The doctors not sued spent on average, five minutes longer with each patient. That's it.

There are actually two points about this I'd like to make. One is that I believe the study shows the patient's willingness to forgive the doctor for his mistakes, when he made them. Because the five minutes of extra time the doctor spent with them conveyed to the patient that he truly "cared" about their well-being.

You probably wouldn't sue a friend and from the results of the study, apparently we don't tend to sue someone who we trust, or we feel cares about us.

Secondly, my question for you. Is five minutes a "little thing," compared to not spending five extra minutes? I submit to you that it is a small thing that is done with obviously a powerful impact.

Is the customer willing to pay a premium (more than the average price) for the product or service?
In the following chapters there are specific examples of companies that charge way above average for their specific products. This shows a willingness for the consumer to pay extra for comparable products/ services and in most cases, it is because of the wonderful experience and remarkable customer service that they provide.

Has the competition tried to emulate a feature or benefit of the product or service because of the success the company has had or because the consumer has demanded it, due to the competition? Many companies would consider this the highest compliment possible. To be copied by their competition because their company is doing something "so right," that it is worth it to do so.

DON'T THINK BIG, THINK SMALL

There are several books that discuss the "small" things in life. I want you to think of small things you can implement that will have a big impact on your business.

At some level, what we provide for our customers is a commodity. At the most competitive levels of doing business everyday, it isn't big things that make a difference, it's the little things.

Have you ever considered the fact that the top five finishers in just about any sport are all very good? In fact, you and I probably would not be fit to be in the same arena with the top five in whatever sport you just imagined. So they are all very good, right? And what is the difference in say first and fifth place? A few strokes, a few seconds, or a few noses. Now, how about the difference, in the prize money of first and fifth place?

In horse racing, a horse is beaten by one "length" and a length is equal to one fifth of a second. Well, in the breeder's cup last fall (Grand Prairie, Texas 2004), the first place prize money was $2,080,000, and fifth place was $120,000. $2,080,000 minus $120,000 equals $1,960,000, divide $1,960,000 by the 4 places (2nd-5th place) and you get $490,000. So the difference in prize money was $490,000 for every one-fifth of a second difference. In the 2005 Masters golf tournament the number of strokes between first and fifth place was eight strokes and the difference in prize money between first and fifth was 1,023,000 (1st place was $1,260,000, 5th place was $237,000). What is that per stroke? $1,023,000 divided by eight equals $127,875 per stroke. And in the fastest growing spectator sport in our country according to *Fox News* (March 12, 2004) and second only to the NFL with 75 million fans, NASCAR, the Daytona 500 February 20, 2005, first place prize money was $1,497,150, second place was $1,106,130. The differential between first and second place? One sixteenth of a second. That is $391,020 for one sixteenth of a second!

The next time you think that the small things you implement or do in your business don't really matter, remember these numbers.

When we do a financial plan for someone, a 1% difference in return over a 20-30 year period makes a huge difference in the amount of wealth and lifestyle our clients can have in their future. On a side note, what is sad is that in a Dalbar (a marketing firm that compiles statistics for the financial services industry) study from 1987 through 1999, investors who used an advisor during these 12 years earned 16% more than people who invested on their own using no load funds.

Unfortunately, almost everyone we interview has had a bad experience with a financial advisor. This causes them to be reluctant to trust anyone new and use our help to improve their financial lives. The real people who lose are the investors because if they can never get past the trust issue, we won't be able to help them, and they won't have the quality of life they deserve.

In *The E Myth Revisited,* Michael Gerber describes a wonderful experience of staying at a hotel called the Venetia, just outside of San Francisco. This hotel has a reputation of doing small things that delight the customer during their stay that is beyond their expectations. He decides to investigate how the experience is replicated with precision every time, for every guest.

The owner shows him an operations manual, (it could be called a customer service agreement). Each employee has a checklist of the things they are to do for each guest. Things like turning on the fireplace so it is lit when the customer retires for the evening. Also, asking each patron which paper they prefer so that particular newspaper is at their door for them in the morning. When the owner describes to Gerber the reputation that his hotel has established, he states, "when people talk about us, it's not the big things they talk about, it's the little things."

Twenty years ago, on a trip I took in Maine, I took a ferry to Monhegan Island. This was more of a taxi which took people to the island which was home for them or people who were going to work for the day on the island. I was going over for a day of exploring. I made friends with the captain and he allowed me to steer the boat. He pointed at the compass and told me to make sure the needle stayed on a certain line on the compass and not to either side of it. I asked him what would happen if the needle was say on the next mark over from where he directed me to steer the boat. This next mark over on the compass was maybe a millimeter. He stated that we would be 100 yards off course if we would waiver to the next closest mark. That really made an impression on me and stuck with me as one of the first times in my life that I realized a small thing can make a big difference.

As I did my research for this book, I realized that the large companies and small local companies, in almost every example, that what sets them apart and makes them remarkable, are the small things they implement that make an emotional impact on their customers.

A CAN OF PAINT

Another example of how small things make a difference has to do with a can of paint. I was at a presentation a few years ago and the presenter was discussing this very topic, small things making a big difference. One of his stories involved a can of paint. Now I don't know the complete history of the paint can. Standard size cans of paint only come in two or three sizes. As you can imagine, there wasn't much research out there about the evolution of the history of the paint can. I mean, I'm 42 years old and my best recollection of my first paint can experience would have probably been when I was around five years old. That means at least for the last 30 some years, the structure and design of a can of paint, has remained unchanged.

So as a child down in our basement, I would tinker around dad's work bench "helping out." Whether it was a school art project that required a coat of paint or freshening up a room in the house, resealing a can of paint was an art in and of itself. I'm sure your own paint can memoirs include putting the lid back on the can of paint. You had to drape a rag over the can of paint so it wouldn't splatter out from the lid as you took a hammer and hammered down on the lid, resealing the paint. You had to hammer down pretty hard to make sure it was air-tight and wouldn't dry up the paint for the next use.

So this process did keep the paint air tight and from drying up but it also caused a problem. The paint that was left around the rim dried, making it harder and messier to reopen the can. The magic tool to re-pry the lid was a small crow bar with a curved edge on one end and a ring for your fingers on the other. To this day, these special tools can be found taped to the sides of paint cans or handed out free at your hardware store.

Isn't it odd that for at least 35 years or so this archaic process has been repeated over and over again in garages and basements all over this country? Isn't it odd that only a few years ago Sherwin-Williams became the first company to change the packaging of a paint can? They put a spout on top of the paint can, which made it more convenient to reseal and reopen and less messy than the conventional method used for over 30 years.

When Sherwin-Williams first introduced the spout paint can, according to the company sales increased dramatically. Clearly the consumer was ready for a different method of storing and reusing paint. Was it an expensive change for the company? No. Were the researchers at Sherwin-Williams brilliant? Hardly. But now that you think of it, you might wonder, "what took them so long?"

Now Sherwin-Williams has been around a long time and I'm sure they have a good product in the paint they produce, but there are a lot of other companies that produce good paint as well. In fact, if you are into the name brand thing, you can even get Ralph Lauren paint. But I seriously doubt if anyone would walk in your home and state, "Wow, you used Ralph Lauren paint, didn't you?"

There are cheap paints that probably don't last very long or don't dry as fast, but in the top five companies in the paint business, wouldn't you think, paint is paint? Sherwin-Williams found a better and easier, less messy way to give the customer what they wanted. And they were rewarded for doing so with increased revenues after the pour spout was introduced.

THE TIPPING POINT

Malcolm Gladwell's *The Tipping Point* revolutionized the way I see my business and the marketing of it. In fact, after reading Gladwell's book, I was asked to speak at a conference hosted by the company I am affiliated with. It was fun experience and the location was Notre Dame University. I was told I could talk about anything I wanted which is almost worse than being given a topic.

That certainly narrowed it down for me; speaking to your peers is often the hardest audience. To be invited to this conference you had to be at a certain point of success within your career. So as I contemplated what did I possibly have to share with these already successful advisors, self-doubt set in. I thought what on earth am I going to tell them that will have a huge impact on their business and make it better. I was thinking large not small. And that was my problem.

Then I remembered Gladwell's book small things becoming tipping points or revolutions because of their impact on a given market or product. I realized there was nothing huge I could tell these already successful advisors. But that isn't what they needed. At some level of success, just like in your business there are a lot of companies that have a good quality product or service. The little things you implement, primarily on how you treat your customer will have the biggest impact.

So it actually helped me with my self-doubt talk. I didn't have to come up with some huge idea to change their businesses. They didn't need that. They needed small ideas that they could implement easily, quickly and even inexpensively to have a positive emotional impact on their customers. That is what you will see from the businesses described in this book and by reading their "stories" and how they impact their customers on an emotional level, you will think of ideas for you in your business to do the same.

XEROX

Do you ever walk into a hotel and say to yourself, "This certainly isn't the Ritz." A good example of this is in your home or office, when you want to make a photo copy of something what do you say? Will you Xerox this for me? I say it all of the time, without thinking about it. That example is almost, not quite as powerful as the Harley tattoo. When I think of photocopying I think of one company, Xerox. I actually am not even thinking at all. My subconscious regurgitates this word that has been burned into my brain, and when I think of photocopy, there Xerox, it pops up again. There are things in our life that our subconscious actually answers for us. At a marketing presentation a few years ago the presenter flashed on the screen the name of a particular company, and we were to speak out loud the tag line that was associated with each company.

TEST

Let's see how you do:
1. 7Up the .....
2. Coke the......
3. Hallmark when you care enough......
4. Winston tastes good like.......
(Answers are at the end of this chapter.)

Almost everyone in the audience could recite the tag line verbatim. That part was interesting, but most of us were shocked when the presenter went on to say that at the time, these commercials hadn't aired for over twenty years!

The reason we were able to pull this from the subconscious level of our brain is because these mega Fortune 500 companies have spent millions of dollars in advertising, making sure that these phrases stuck in our brain. In Malcolm Gladwell's book *The Tipping Point*, he refers to this as the "stickiness factor." A message that sticks in your head that you can't get rid of, even if you wanted to.

THE DIFFERENCE TODAY IN EFFECTIVE MARKETING

The problem today with the "stickiness factor" is that almost nothing sticks in our head anymore. Today we have to be continually flooded with the same message over and over more so than in the past and even then, advertisers are learning that it is not as effective as it used to be. The return on premium for the advertising dollar today is so low that many companies have found it is not effective to rely on the traditional methods of advertising, television, radio and print advertising.

To get a message to stick today, there has to be an emotional tie and a passionate experience, enough so that the consumer who participates in the customer experience spreads a story.

MILLION DOLLAR MARKETING BUDGET

Now, I'm sure that most people reading this book don't have a million dollars to throw at advertising every year. But let me ask you, if you did would you use expensive television ads like these companies did, or would you use that money to make small changes to your business that wow your customers into advocates for you, creating advocate marketing?

I like to play the game, "if money wasn't an object." I have hired personal consultants and business coaches over the years and somewhere along the way one of them shared this concept with me. When it comes to planning your business strategy or marketing strategy, you first make your plan realistic. Then you ask yourself, "If money wasn't an object, what would I do?"

This helps you stretch your goals and your mind to consider what you would really want to do, given adequate resources to do it. Mentally preparing yourself for what would be the next best thing you could implement with less funding or for the future, when your resources are greater.

We can go back to the question in a minute. I'd like for you to consider something as you contemplate how you would spend your millions. In our business, financial advising, I have heard over and over again how 80% of the production is done by 20% of the advisors in our company. In fact our company got wise and a few years ago, they took the top 20% and even put us in a group and gave us a name, The Sterling Group. They also gave us our own toll-free number to reach a special department for every product and service we provide for our clients.

I'm sure that this was an expensive change and continues to be. But they recognize where 80% of the business in the company comes from and so are applying more resources towards this group. In *The Tipping Point,* Gladwell refers to this as the law of the few. He comments that this is how sociable, energetic and influential people can cause products like Hush Puppies to go from being worn only by fashionable New Yorkers, to being sold in malls all over the country.

ADVOCATE MARKETING IMPOSTERS (BUZZ MARKETING)

One more point before we get back to our question. I read somewhere that marketing firms for various products are actually paying adults to pose as teenagers and log in to teen chat rooms and talk about a new product. The adult, posing as the teen would excitedly talk about the new product, how great it was and how "everyone who is anyone," should try it.

Now, I think this is a little unethical, but apparently legal, but what were they in effect doing? The adult posing as a child was also "posing" as an advocate, for a certain music CD or other product. I call this an advocate marketing imposter.

The marketing company's hope was that this word-of-mouth advertising would spread to the other advocates who were on line. I would have to think that this is undoubtedly a very inexpensive way to advertise. But obviously, these marketing firms saw enough value in the process to spend time and money doing it.

TREMOR

Well, before I could finish this book, it happened. A company was sued for a version of doing what I have just described for you. According to *USA Today*, Proctor and Gamble the world's biggest packaged goods marketer was sued by the consumer advocacy group, Commercial Alert. Commercial Alert filed a complaint with the Federal Trade Commission stating that P & G's word-of-mouth marketing unit targets teens with deceptive advertising.

The marketing unit for P & G is appropriately titled Tremor. It is a four-year-old division of P & G and has a panel of 250,000 teens ages 13 to 19 of which 75% are female. The sole purpose of these 250,000 panelists is to talk with their friends about new products or concepts P & G sends them. In return the teens receive free product samples. According to Steve Knox CEO of Tremor, the kids receive something else for being a panelist, "to be a member is empowering for a teen." "You have a voice that will be heard, and you get cool information before your friends receive it."

Marian Salzman, trend spotter at JWT Worldwide, estimates that more than 85% of the nations top 1,000 marketers now use some form of this kind of advertising. What is interesting to me when I interviewed a local ad agency is that they wouldn't deny or admit that they suggested this form of advertising. When I asked what it was called, they stated it didn't really have a name, but it was like "blogging."

Advertising Age titles this form of advertising "buzz marketing."

So it appears that the media have given it a name. And according to *Advertising Age*, it is estimated to be a $100 million to $150 million industry and one of the highest growth areas of marketing.

Blogging is a cyber space version of word of mouth marketing. In the May 2002 issue of *Wired,* an article by Andrew Sullivan describes blogging as "changing the media world." He goes on to say blogging is to words what Napster was to music, except this time there is nothing illegal. Blogging is a place for people to write and discuss any variety of topics and get feedback from hundreds, thousands, even millions of readers. What better place for marketing companies to go to find out what the consumer thinks of their products and services. And again, posing as an advocate for a particular product, the employee paid by the marketing company can be given a script of what to say to elicit readers to want to go out and try the products and services that they are trying to market. Again, this is an advocate marketing imposter.

What is so interesting is that in both of these methods described, very large corporations are implementing these strategies into their actual marketing plans to try and infest the marketplace with the idea that whatever they are trying to sell, is great and you and I can't possibly live without it. Now Andrew Sullivan is an accomplished writer with a good fan base, but even knowing that, it is still amazing that in twenty-one months he has compiled a quarter of a million readers a month on his website.

NOW BACK TO THE QUESTION

If you had a million dollar marketing budget how would you spend it? Throwing all you can at an advertising firm to develop a television commercial for you might sound like the easiest answer. But let me ask you to consider, have you ever seen a Starbucks ad on television or heard one on the radio? How about Ritz-Carlton? Now, I suppose I could have "missed" them, but I don't think so. So why is that? Two very successful companies that have a different idea of marketing.

They are creating advocates, by the experiences they provide.

Regardless of where you live, you've no doubt seen Starbucks at fund raising events or charity walks in your community. I have, and I'm sure that is a way for them to advertise. This conveys they care about the community and are giving back to the community. It's hard not to like a company that does that. And while doing so, continue to create passion in their customers.

When your customer thinks of whatever it is you can provide for them, you want them to think of you over your competition. You can do this by eliciting emotions created by the experience you give them, when they do business with your company. That ultimate customer experience provides passion and emotion that create your advocates. By producing many advocates for your business you then have advocate marketing.

How do the companies in this book accomplish that experience? And what do you do or implement to create it for you, your company and your customers?

Answers to test:
1. ...the un-cola
2. ...the real thing
3. ...to send the very best
4. ...a cigarette should

How did you do?

Notes:

CHAPTER THREE

WHY NOW?

"The ultimate of being successful is the luxury of giving yourself the time to do what you want to do."
— Leontyne Price
18 time Grammy award winner and opera singer (1970's to 1985)

"Time is really the only capital that any human being has, and the only thing he can't afford to loose."
— Thomas Edison
inventor of the first commercially practical incandescent electric light bulb in 1879

"Time is the deposit each one has in the bank of God and no one knows the balance."
— Ralph Sockman
American author famous for his leadership quotes

- **Mass advertising**: It is getting harder and harder to stand out among your competition. Remember the 1975 grocery store with only 3,200 products on their shelves versus today's 64,000? Or the 3,000 ads a year that our parents were exposed to that is now 5,000 a day? It is getting harder and harder to stand out among all of the "noise."

  Have you ever looked at CNN or MSNBC? There are multiple

companies with ads on every screen of that form of news. I'm sure you don't want to be reminded of the pop up ads on your computer everyday, when you try and access the internet. We have desensitized ourselves to ignore most of what we see and hear in the form of advertising. We long for that personal touch of someone, who already knows us so well and what we want, we don't even have to ask for it. We want things personalized or customized for us, not what just everyone else has. We want this because most of us have an inherent desire to feel special or unique.

- **Competition**: If you look around you there are plenty of businesses that offer the same product or service you do. And I'll bet they probably do a pretty good job of it too. In my industry for example, there are plenty of great financial services firms to choose from. And today you can walk into a bank, and buy the same products and services, that we provide for our clients. So I ask myself all of the time what it is that I do differently and better than anyone else to earn my client's business. Did I do something to make my client feel special and taken care of? Did I customize the service for the client? Did I save my client time, so he or she could focus on what is important to him/her in their life?

- **Time**: I read once that we have about sixty thousand thoughts per day and most of them are random. Also, many of our thoughts are negative and are similar to thoughts we have had in the past. This coupled with the exposure to 5,000 pleas for our dollar everyday, or the 64,000 products to select in the average grocery store, no wonder our minds are on overload. How can we possibly squeeze into our consumer's mind a positive experience that won't take up more of their valuable time?

Additionally, with email and the use of the Internet we have become more productive than any other generation. But because we can do more in an eight-hour day, we create more work for ourselves. People often take work home to finish whatever wasn't finished at the office. This causes us to have less quality time to spend with our loved ones or our hobbies and interests. Because of this any time you can save the client time, as long as your product or service is of good quality, you will get the business.

- **We are a service country**: I heard a money manager speak once, and he said that we don't really produce anything in this country anymore. We are all service people serving other service people. Most of our products today are imported. It is often cheaper for us to ship parts of a product to be assembled in a foreign country, and then pay to have the completed product shipped back to us and still save money. That is incredible to comprehend. Whether we like the situation or not, that is the way many companies in our country choose to do business to remain profitable in today's marketplace.

  Did you know that according to *Fortune Magazine* (fortune.com, 2005 Global 500, July 12, 2005) that 9 of the 10 largest engineering firms; 9 of the 10 largest electronics companies; 8 of the 10 largest automakers; 7 of the 10 largest banks and 6 of the 10 largest food and drug stores are not located in the United States? We are a service country.

- **The baby boomer generation**: Over the next twenty years, you and I have a huge opportunity to grow our businesses with great customer service. 12,000 baby boomers turn 50 every day, and they reach age 60 to the tune of one every 7 seconds. The boomer generation numbers can vary and I realize the exact number will depend on what or who directs you to the boomer numbers. But according to the U.S. Census Bureau, between 1946 and 1964 there were 75.8 million of us born. And let's not forget immigration over the last 40 years. Even if you think the number is as low as say, 65 million, and I doubt anyone knows the exact number anyway, if you do the math on 65 million, one will turn 60 every seven seconds starting now and ending in 15 years.

This isn't just the largest group of consumers to be walking around the good old U.S.A., but the most affluent, as well. This generation receives much publicity about its numbers and volume. But why shouldn't it? It is the generation that stretched the public school system in the '60's. Then stretched inflation rates in the '70's. It elevated housing levels to new high's in the '80's. And if you aren't old enough to remember any of those eras, I'm sure everyone reading this book can remember the economic and stock boom of the 90's. Harry Dent, respected economist, author, and a man who has spent 25 years studying trends in our economy, describes such trends in his book, *The Great Boom Ahead*. Dent comments on the boomers impact on our future; "This huge generation of consumers will drive the greatest economic boom in our history." Dent goes on to say that the boomer generation, as a group of consumers, is "like a pig moving through a python."

I hope I have made a reasonable plea with you, so that you at least agree, that the more customer advocates you create, the more business you will generate, the more fun you will have producing the income you need, and you will have more time to spend with the people and things you love. And creating advocates for your business (advocate marketing) could not come at a better time, than now.

Notes:

_____

_____

_____

_____

_____

_____

_____

_____

_____

_____

_____

_____

_____

_____

_____

_____

_____

_____

_____

CHAPTER FOUR

19,000 Ways

"There is nothing more difficult to take in hand, more perilous to conduct, or more uncertain in its success than to take the lead in introducing a new order of things."
— **Machiavelli**
Italian patriot and political genius (1500-1527)

"If the rate of change on the outside exceeds the rate of change on the inside, the end is near."
— **Jack Welch**
CEO of General Electric and credited with turning the company around, currently a consultant to fortune 500 companies

"I don't focus on where the puck is but on where it is going."
— **Wayne Gretzky**
Professional hockey player

I'll tell you what 19,000 represents later on, and you will see why it is one of those statistics you hear that makes you say, "What?" If you think consumers don't want customization or personalization in the product or service you have to offer, by the end of this chapter, certainly you will remember that number, 19,000.

First, let's do a quick study of customization. At Arby's, the fast food restaurant known for its roast beef sandwich, thirty years ago had one roast beef sandwich; today the chain has seven sandwiches that are strictly roast beef. Not to mention the five tortilla wraps and ten other types of sandwiches, not including salads and breakfast! The ice cream company Dreyer's, has 250 different flavors of ice cream and Frito-Lay, the "chip" company, has sixty kinds of chips. Minute Maid orange juice also had one selection of OJ thirty years ago; today—no pulp, extra pulp, vitamin C enriched, low acid, kids plus, original plus calcium, country style, home squeezed style, home squeezed with calcium and vitamin D, and, of course, original. And that doesn't include the OJ that is mixed with other fruits, which makes a grand total of twenty-four different juices. I rest my case on what the consumer wants today. How else did the average grocery store go from 3,200 products on their shelves in 1975 to 64,000 today?

But the granddaddy of customization is 19,000. Let me paint a picture for you: as you walk in the door, you hear pleasing music, and more than one person usually will eagerly ask "How can I help you today?" or "What can I get for you today?" The selection to choose from is hung high on a sign above the counter, with big bold letters, so you can easily select from the menu of choices. And what an array of choices: five different sizes—Grande, Venti, Solo, Doppio (whatever that is!), and six ounces; four different choices of "milk;" twenty-five different types of condiments, not to mention the twenty-eight different flavors of coffee; all made to order, plus whip, no whip foam, no foam, which in themselves would double the number of possible scenarios.

When you input all of the possibilities into a computer to see how many ways you can actually make a cup of coffee, according to the company themselves, you come up with the magic number, 19,000. Is there really any way that you could think of making your own special cup of Joe, that wouldn't be included in those 19,000? I would doubt it. So that is why, I call Starbucks the ultimate in the quest for the customization of a product. By the way, these flavors and ingredients, along with all of the nutritional information on all of their products, can be looked up on the company's website. And none of the 19,000 considers all of the variations for a cup of tea.

Starbucks also continues to implement small, progressive changes in the way they serve their customer to keep customers coming back. And not just for a cup of coffee, but to be engaged in the ambiance of a truly delightful, relaxed and time-saving experience.

AWARDS

As I researched the company, I learned many other aspects that re-affirmed my suspicions, that this highly successful company is doing all of the right things to maintain its success. Here are a few of their accolades. Recognized as one of the "Ten Most Admired Companies in America" *Fortune* magazine, 2003. One of "The 100 Best Companies to Work For" *Fortune* 1998, 1999, 2000, 2002, 2003 and 2004. "Most Admired Company" in the food service category, *Fortune* 2001 and 2002. BrandChannel.com named Starbucks "Top Five" in "Reader's Choice 2001 Brand of the Year Award" March 2002. And among its peers in the restaurant and food service, Howard Schultz is recognized as one of the "Top Six Entrepreneurs of the Year" *Restaurant Business* March 2001.

And it isn't just in the U.S. that Starbucks is admired. They were named "Best Product of the Year" in Korea, *Joongang Daily Newspaper*, December 2000, and "Number One Restaurant Chain," in Tokyo, Japan, *Nikkei Restaurant* magazine, July 2000. The French have always seen the U. S. coffee as weak, and refer to it as "jus chaussette," which means sock juice. So for them to open their first store in 2004, it was considered a challenge because of how the French perceive our "sock juice."

PHILANTHROPY

When it comes to philanthropy and ethics Starbucks shines in that arena as well. One of "100 Best Corporate Citizens," *Business Ethics* magazine, 2000, 2001, 2002. The "Corporate Citizenship Award" for various community service programs, Citizen Fund, April 19, 2000. The "National Leadership Award" for philanthropic and educational efforts to battle AIDS, AIDS Action, Washington D. C., April 5, 1999. I hope you don't feel I'm trying to beat a dead horse here, and just so you know, I am not naming all the awards this company has received. You can go to their website www.starbucks.com, and see a complete listing. I am naming enough, however, to show the company's credibility and also illustrate the many different areas where the company has received awards.

So forgive me, but I'd like to name just a few more in this category. One of "The Best Companies to Work for in America for People with Disabilities" *WE Magazine*, May 24, 1997. "The Stafford Award for Corporate Leadership" in recognition of the company's sensitive reuse of older spaces within our cities, *Scenic America* May 13, 1997. The 1996 "Corporate Conscience Award for International Human Rights," Council on Economic Priorities June 4, 1996. And lastly, the 1996 International Humanitarian Award, CARE May 10, 1996.

Let's explore Starbucks mission statement to further discover the guiding principles that help establish the company's esteemed status among its peers.

MISSION STATEMENT

The Starbucks mission statement is: Established as the premier Purveyor of the finest coffee in the world, while maintaining our uncompromising principles while we grow. **To do this Starbucks has six guiding principles:**
1. Provide a great work environment and treat each other with respect and dignity.
2. Embrace diversity as an essential component in the way we do business.
3. Apply the highest standards of excellence to the purchasing, roasting and fresh delivery of our coffee.

4. Develop enthusiastically satisfied customers (develop advocates, my addition), all of the time.
5. Contribute positively to our communities and our environment.
6. Recognize that profitability is essential to our future success.

ENVIRONMENTAL MISSION STATEMENT

Starbucks also has an environmental mission statement, as the company sees itself as an environmental leader. **The five principles for their environmental mission are:**
1. Understanding of environmental issues and sharing information with our partners.
2. Developing innovative and flexible solutions to bring about change.
3. Striving to buy, sell, and use environmentally friendly products.
4. Recognizing that fiscal responsibility is essential to our environmental future.
5. Encouraging all partners to share in our mission.

It's clear what Starbucks is striving for, and you are the judge if they have attained and continue to attain their goal. We can all learn and implement ideas from this highly successful company, to make our own products and services better.

EMPLOYEES AS PARTNERS

In the area of employee relations, Starbucks calls the people they hire "partners" and openly states that their "ability to accomplish what we set out to do is based primarily on the people we hire." The company is always focused on their people and providing opportunities for them to develop their skills, further their career and achieve their personal goals. They emphasize respect in how they treat each other and their customers. The type of employee they want to hire are self-motivated, passionate (there is that word I love again), creative team players. Realizing that the right people offering their ideas and expertise will enable them to continue their success.

PASSION

One Starbucks district manager defined the atmosphere Starbucks is striving to create as, "What makes Starbucks different is our passion for what we do. We're trying to provide a great experience for people, with a great product. That's what we all care about."

Starbucks doesn't just give lip service on how genuine they are about their feelings for their employees. In 1991, they were the first privately-owned U.S. company to offer a stock option program that includes part-time employees.

In my business and the many different people I encounter, I can attest to the wealth that stock options provide for people in this country. I can recall some of my associates in the mid 1990s in Austin, Texas, describing how their clients who were $40,000 year salaried administrative assistants at Dell computer who became millionaires almost over night, due to their stock options.

Personally, at two different times, I used my stock options to pay cash for both of my Harley Davidson motorcycles. And in 2004 alone, the company I am affiliated with, awarded $64 million in stock options.

EMPLOYEES CAN WORK ON THEIR SCHEDULE

I wanted to interview an employee of Starbucks to try and get an understanding of why the employees I encounter seem to be so darn happy. I went to a local Starbucks and talked with one of the employees. I simply asked him, "Why do you like working here?"

I'll never forget his response, he said "This company cares about me." I asked him if he knew that according to the company themselves they are the largest retail chain in the world based on the number of customers they serve each week. So I told him I was very curious why he felt the largest retail chain in the world cared about one single employee on University Drive in Fort Worth Texas.

He told me that he was a student at Texas Christian University, but he was from Amarillo Texas. He stated that his father would disown him if he didn't come home every summer and work the family farm. Previous jobs he had in school didn't allow him to take off for the summer and have a job waiting for him in the fall when he returned. He mentioned that it was very stressful to have the pressure of finding a new job every fall. But Starbucks allowed him to take the summer off and he felt they valued him enough to guarantee a job for him in the fall when he came back to school.

In this way Starbucks caters to its employees' desires. These smart, educated college students are allowed to work during the school year, take the summer "off" and come back in the fall and start right back to work when they are ready. Starbucks knows that it costs money to train new employees and realizes that students from out of state, might want to go home and be with their family over the summer or might be taking a college course overseas for the summer time. So to accommodate their student employees, they let them have time off to do these kinds of activities and welcome them back when school starts. The flexibility is good for the student workers as they feel valued and don't have to have the stress of finding a new job after summer is over.

Other employers might not allow such flex-time and so would discourage students from working at other establishments. This policy is good for Starbucks as they can hire part time summer help and have their experienced help back in the fall to take over responsibilities, and Starbucks doesn't incur more cost of training someone new in the fall. If a student starts out in their sophomore or junior year, with the average stay at a university for undergraduate only, being five years today, that is several years of keeping a good employee. With graduate and doctorate studies, their tenure could be even longer. Consider that these educated young people buy in to Starbucks the company, because Starbucks was flexible for them while they were receiving their higher education. Add to that the opportunity for them to purchase stock through a stock option program, which only further ingrained in their young impressionable minds, that this was truly a company that cared about their future. What is the result for Starbucks when these young, successful future businessmen and women go out into the world as investors? The continued potential for these former students and employees, to buy more and more shares of Starbucks' stock. Not a bad outcome for a company with a simple idea, "why not allow part-time employees to own shares of the company, through stock options?"

NOT JUST A CUP OF JOE

In 2001, Starbucks started offering high-speed wireless internet access in stores. A colleague of mine uses Starbucks in his daily course of business, in his words, "because they are everywhere." Throughout his day as he goes to his small business clients, he stops at Starbucks to check his email, make phone calls and communicate with his staff via the internet. Not a bad way of using them as a resource, and since most stores have internet access, he knows that once he sees the familiar green and white sign up ahead on the road, he can plan one of his stops.

A FORWARD THINKING COMPANY

Another creative idea as it relates to serving the customer and giving them what they want is the reloadable credit card Starbucks introduced in 1991. This allows consumers to pay in advance when they possibly have the cash for future purchases. And it can be "reloaded" in the convenience of their home or office on the internet, as well as in the store. To add even more benefit to their reloadable card, in 2003, Starbucks came out with the "Starbucks Card Duetto Visa." This was the first-of-its-kind payment card, blending Visa credit card functionality, with their reloadable card.

In 1993, Starbucks started its partnership with Barnes and Noble Inc. bookstores. This allowed the customer to sip on a cup of coffee in the bookstore, while reviewing a book or magazine to potentially purchase.

In 2004, Starbucks launched a in-store CD burning service to create a new music delivery experience so customers can create customized CDs. They title this service "Starbucks Hear Music."

Starbucks has been in the U.S. since 1971, opening its first store in Seattle Washington. They first entered Europe in 1998. Today they have 400 outlets in the United Kingdom, and 900 stores in Europe all together. There are over 270 stores in Canada and a total of 18,000 stores outside the U.S. And speaking of another statistical number that makes you say "wow," Starbucks serves 25 million customers each week, and according to the company themselves, makes it the largest retailer in the world. Not bad for basically serving you one small item, a hot cup of coffee.

As innovative and forward thinking as Starbucks is as a company, I can't wait to see what they come up with next.

How Starbucks addresses the ten attributes of advocate marketing:

- **Differentiating factor:** multiple ways to create your own cup of coffee, in the store or on the go through the drive through, and experience it with the "Duetto Visa" card. High speed internet access for keeping in touch with business and friends and the "Hear Music," CD burning service.
- **Customer loyalty:** "Twenty-five million customers per week making it the largest retailer in the world."
- **Saving the Customer Time:** Drive through service, high speed wireless internet access," ability to "reload" Starbucks card "online at home or the office," "sip a cup of coffee while reviewing a book or magazine to potentially buy."
- **Customer "experience" so a "story" is told about the company:** Allowing college student workers to benefit from the stock option program and to allow them to take the summer off, with a guaranteed job waiting for them when school starts again.
- **Create customization in your product or service:** "19,000 ways" says it all.
- **Employees feel apart of the company:** "are always focused on

their people and providing opportunities for them to develop their skills," "calls the people they hire "partners," "encouraging all partners to share in our mission." "In 1991, they were the first privately owned U.S. company to offer a stock option program that includes part-time employees." "College students are allowed to work during the school year, take the summer "off" and come back in the fall and start right back to work."

- **The forgiveness factor:** Ok, you have me on this one. I couldn't find an example where forgiveness was needed as it pertains to Starbucks. Maybe it is because they are so darn good at what they do, it is rarely needed. I submit however, that when a mistake is made on an order for example, their loyal customers would forgive them.
- **Is the customer willing to pay a premium?** $7.50 for a cup of coffee, a product that in most metropolitan areas can be found for $2, that is a 275% mark up.
- **Does the competition try and emulate products or features of the company:** Well, one comment here is based on the word "latte" that is used in a seminar we do that is adapted from the book *Smart Women Finish Rich* by David Bach who uses the term "latte factor" to describe how just spending $3 a day on investments for oneself versus on a $3 cup of coffee, can make an impact on the wealth someone accumulates. This book has been very popular and a New York Times bestseller over the last several years.

The term "latte factor" has stuck and is sometimes used in our industry as a way to get clients to consider where they are spending their money as it relates to where they want to be financially. The author would not have been able to use this term, prior to Starbucks' success, as it would not have had the same impact.

Think of your community now and ten years ago. Ten years ago, you probably had breakfast places that served coffee, but few coffee shops that only served coffee. Today, all around towns from my observation, the coffee shop as a way of embracing sitting and enjoying a cup of coffee as the primary reason for the business, is relatively new to the younger set of our culture. Starbucks has definitely had influence in our culture, and the way we think about our coffee. And thanks to this forward thinking, progressive company, we can have it served to us, 19,000 ways.

- **Don't think big, think small:** Allowing students to work during the school year, take the summer off and have their job waiting for them when school starts again. A small example that causes an employee in one small individual store to feel cared about by the largest retail chain in the world—*amazing!*

Notes:

_____

_____

_____

_____

_____

_____

_____

_____

_____

_____

_____

_____

_____

_____

_____

_____

_____

_____

_____

_____

CHAPTER FIVE

PUTTIN' ON THE RITZ

"A man's success in business today turns upon his power of getting people to believe he has something that they want."
— **Gerald Stanley Lee**
Author of inspirational quotes and stories

"There are two things to aim at in life: first to get what you want: and after that, to enjoy it. Only the wisest of mankind achieve the second."
— **Logan Pearsall Smith**
Anglo-American author

Have you ever stayed at a Ritz-Carlton resort, or known someone who has? There is a story to tell isn't there? If you haven't experienced it yet, you need to go once, and you will know what I am talking about. I also will challenge you, when you come back from your experience, try not to tell a story about it. I will bet that you will have to stop yourself from wanting to tell anyone who will listen, how wonderful it was.

After my own experience, and the fact that everyone I have ever known who has stayed at a Ritz always wants to share their story about how amazing it was, I wanted to research this company because of its appeal to its customers. Since the organization has attained mystique status, how did they fare when one considers them and the ten essentials for customer advocates and advocate marketing?

PERSONAL EXPERIENCE

On a business trip a few years ago, I had the opportunity to experience the Ritz-Carlton. I had heard of their reputation and their being known for the first class way they treat their customers. And similar to the Harley owner who said if you don't own one, you won't "get it," you need to stay at a Ritz at least one time to really appreciate what their operation is all about.

My trip started with a flight into San Francisco and my driver picking me up at the airport. Now, I don't normally have a driver pick me up, but this was a special company awards trip and we were going to the Ritz-Carlton. As we headed north from the airport, I sat in the back seat and enjoyed the beautiful California countryside as we headed for the Ritz-Carlton at Half Moon Bay. As we pulled into the circle drive in front of the hotel, there was a line of cars in front of us dropping off passengers. As the car slowed to a stop, the bellman opened the door and said, "Welcome to the Ritz-Carlton, Miss Turner."

I was stunned as to how he already knew my name. I could see the line of cars behind me waiting their turn to drop off their passengers, and those cars looked pretty much like the one I was in. I never noticed the driver use his cell phone to call in letting the bellman know who I was. So how did he know that I was in this particular car?

Looking back now, I wish I would have asked, but I didn't, so I can't tell you. But I can tell you that was just the beginning of my wonderful experience at the Ritz and why myself and many others based on the company's awards and repeat customers, believe the Ritz-Carlton hotels have earned their place as the premier provider of luxury lodging services in the world (The Luxury Institute, 2005).

As I walked through the hotel, literally every employee would turn and welcome me as if I was royalty or someone famous. And by the end of my stay, I truly felt like I was. This particular hotel had the look and feel of Scotland. It was dusk and the fog was rolling off the ocean. As I walked outside to the back of the hotel, I looked up to my right, and I could see one of the greens of the golf course, and behind it, the fairway that sloped up to the top of the hill. With the history of golf starting in Scotland, I thought, "What a perfect setting."

I went back in and a driver offered to take me around to my bungalow. After getting my things situated in my room, I was about to go back out again, and I heard music that made me stop. I opened my door and looked back toward the main part of the hotel, and there on the hill was a lone bag pipe player, complete with plaid kilt, playing music as the sun was setting over the ocean. If I didn't think I was in Scotland before, that certainly did it! This routine happened every night at dusk during my stay. I shook my head and went back inside wondering "What they would think of next?"

I decided to freshen up before heading out for dinner. I am used to the normal amenities associated with high quality hotels, but as I was leaving the bathroom, a card placed on a stack of towels on the bathtub caught my eye. It read: If you would like to have your bath drawn for you, dial extension ## on your phone. Now I have stayed in some of the nicest hotels in this country such as the Waldorf, Le Meridian and others, but I have never seen an offer like that!

My mischievous side wanted to dial that extension just to see who would show up, but I decided I didn't quite need that much pampering! But part of the fun was, I could have.

NOT ALLOWED TO POINT

Now that I have read more about the company and how it has become the ultimate in vacation experiences, I look back on my trip and see why the Ritz-Carlton has earned its well deserving mystique. Did you know Ritz-Carlton employees are not allowed to point? Indeed, the customer is always first, and second is the specific duty assigned as an employee of the Ritz-Carlton.

I experienced this myself during my stay. I was walking down the hallway towards the pool and I had a good idea where I was going, so I wasn't planning on stopping to ask anyone. But as I entered this hallway, there was an employee watering a plant in the hall. As soon as he noticed me, he stopped watering the plant, put his watering can down, and asked how he could help me. I explained that I was going to the pool and he said, "Let me show you where it is." So he escorted me to the pool and there he asked "Is there anything else I can help you with?" I told him no, and thanked him for his time. Now that is a very small thing to do, but also one of the reasons the patrons of this establishment comment on being treated like royalty. After all, which is more important, treating the paying customers like royalty or watering the plants?

According to Ritz-Carlton's own statistics, on average over a lifetime, its loyal customers spend $250,000 staying at the Ritz. So for the employees, as long as your job gets done, it makes sense, doesn't it, to put the customer first? But there is a reason that the service at the Ritz is so highly regarded. It is because it is rare!

I'm sure that when you think about your own experiences, you agree that service that spoils you to the point of creating the feeling that you are royalty is rare indeed. In fact, imagine for a moment that every time your customer entered your establishment, they were treated this way.

In today's world, it would be remarkable to be treated this way, given the state of many companies and their customer service.

I believe that the Ritz-Carlton "gets it." They know that the consumer today has a strong desire to feel welcomed, to feel special and important. In our fast paced world today, they also want a memorable experience. So memorable that time will stand still for them, with an emotionally positive experience that continues past the duration of their stay. And it would need to when the bill for your stay is several hundred dollars a day, the customer better be walking out saying to themselves "It was worth it." But the ticket price for a night at the Ritz is not just for a night's stay or even for the elegant décor and fine dining, for many luxury hotels have that. You are paying for an emotional experience, that creates the feeling you are special and if not royalty, the next thing to it.

AWARDS

Let me point out that the Ritz is the only company in its category to win the prestigious Malcolm Baldridge award. And they did it not once, but twice, in 1992 and 1999, making it the only service company to win it more than once.

On a quick note, the Baldridge award was established in 1987 and is named after the U.S. Secretary of Commerce who served from 1981 until his tragic death in 1987. Baldridge believed that high quality management and exemplary service would insure America's prosperity and place in world leadership. Congress established this award in 1987 with the predominant criteria: An organization must deliver ever-improving value to customers and improve the organization's overall performance.

But the Baldridge isn't the Ritz's only award. In fact, since the Ritz's incorporation in 1983, The Ritz-Carlton Hotel Company, L.L.C. has received all six of the major awards the hospitality industry and leading consumer organizations can bestow.

J.D. Power and Associates, a global marketing information services firm which bases its awards on surveys of millions of customers internationally, named in 2003 the Ritz-Carlton "Highest in Guest Satisfaction Among Luxury Hotel Chains." The Ritz-Carlton led in each measure of guest satisfaction. In the two years prior, it had placed second competing for the top spot with Four Seasons, Fairmont Hotels and Resorts, and Intercontinental Hotels.

The Ritz-Carlton merits fourth place ranking among the "strongest brands in the world," according to Gerard van Grinsven, Vice President and General Manager of the Ritz-Carlton of Dearborn, Michigan. His hotel received the most improved hotel in the Ritz system in 2002 by the Gallup organization.

Here are just a few of the awards Ritz-Carlton received in 2004:
* Mobil Five-Star Award—6 hotels
* AAA Five Diamond Award—30 hotels
* *Travel and Leisure*: 500 Greatest Hotels in the World—35 hotels

- *Consumer Reports*—No. 1 luxury hotel company, areas including—value, service, upkeep and problem resolution
- *Forbes*: Sure to Impress Travel Destination—Best Hotel Chain
- CNN Ultimate Service Awards—2 hotels
- Worlds Best Hotel Dining Rooms—5 hotels
- *Robb Report*: Best of the Best—3 hotels
- *Travel and Leisure*: World's Best Service Readers Survey—7 hotels
- *Travel and Leisure*: World's Best Business Hotels—8 hotels
- *Conde Nast Traveler*, Top 100 Golf Resorts in North America and the Caribbean—9 hotels
- Wine Spectator Award—18 hotels
- Korean Standard Association Service Award
- The Best Employer in Latin America
- The Best Employer Branding in Singapore Award

CESAR RITZ

How this company began is an interesting story in itself. The hotelier Cesar Ritz, known as "the king of hoteliers and hotelier to kings," was associated with the most renowned hotels of his day, the Grand Hotel in Monte Carlo, the Savoy in London, and then as manager of the Ritz in Paris, starting in 1898 and the Carlton in London, in 1906. Those last two hotel names combined give us the Ritz-Carlton name.

Cesar Ritz established the benchmark for luxury hotels in Europe. He was specific about what he wanted, including things like white walls in guest rooms so no un-cleanliness would go undetected. He was known for comments like: "Never say no when a client asks for something, even if it is for the moon. You can always try." Cesar selected the now recognizable logo, a royal crown symbolic of the British royal seal and the lion, which signifies a financial backer emphasizing the image of wealth.

Cesar died in 1918, but his wife Marie continued expansion of his hotels. In 1927, the Ritz-Carlton moved across the Atlantic, and the Ritz-Carlton in Boston was born. Even though the Ritz opened in many other major cities, only the Boston Ritz survived the Great Depression. The Boston hotel was kept alive by its founder, Edward Wyner. When asked how he kept the hotel alive through this economic downturn, history states that Edward knew he had to keep the aura of success that the Ritz-Carlton was known for. In order to do this, he kept the lights on in vacant rooms, to imply full occupancy.

AHEAD OF ITS TIME

The Boston Ritz-Carlton was ahead of its time in offering service standards unprecedented in American hotel history. Now most luxury hotels offer these amenities that were started by the Ritz: a private bath in guest rooms; elevated dress codes—black tie for Maitre d' and morning suits for all other staff and white tie and apron for waiters and waitresses; smaller intimate lobbies when at the time the customary expansive lobbies were very loud and not conducive to private conversation or privacy.

WORLDWIDE PRESENCE

In 1983, the Ritz-Carlton Boston was sold and the Ritz-Carlton Hotel Company was born. Since then, as of 2004, there are now 57 hotels worldwide who display the Ritz-Carlton logo. The hotels and resorts stretch from the U.S. to China, Singapore and countries you might not expect, like Malaysia, employing 28,000 people worldwide.

In 1998, The Marriot Corporation purchased the Ritz-Carlton. But as guests know, the elegance, perfection and high quality service remains constant from hotel to hotel.

When someone shares a story about the Ritz, high class and elegance that have become the trademark of the Ritz-Carlton are not the most talked about feature. What seems to inspire the most stories is the over-the-top service and the way the customer is spoiled to the point of feeling much as I did, royalty.

As I researched the hiring and training of staff at the Ritz, I could tell that the process and the employees who carry out the experience of the "customer is king," is key to their overwhelming success. In fact, according to *Expert* magazine, the Ritz has the lowest turnover rate of any hotel in the industry.

EMPLOYEES ARE "SELECTED"

According to Gerard van Grinsven, vice-president and area manager for the Ritz-Carlton in Dearborn Michigan, at the Ritz-Carlton, you are not hired you are "selected." This establishment attracts employees to want to work for it. Van Grinsven noted that when he opened the Seoul, Korea, Ritz-Carlton, there were 580 positions available with 15,000 applications.

As far as the screening process for a career at the Ritz, educational background varies with the position. But once hired, the hotel encourages and supports the pursuit of degrees and provides tuition reimbursement for college level work. The Ritz also encourages diversity when hiring. Van Grinsven from the Ritz in Dearborn can identify twenty-two nationalities.

EMPLOYEE EMPOWERMENT

The Ritz is known for setting standards and according to Van Grinsven, the term "empowerment" originated with the Ritz-Carlton. To back up their words with actions, the Ritz-Carlton allows every employee the authority to allocate up to $2,000 of resources for solving a customer's problem immediately, without a supervisor's approval. With this kind of empowerment employees are truly involved in creating the remarkable experience of the Ritz and what it has come to stand for. I also think it would be rare, when giving an employee this kind of empowerment, to hear a Ritz-Carlton employee utter the words, "It's not my job."

Each employee has a rigorous training regimen to prepare them for a job at the Ritz, as well as an annual recertification. The hotel also encourages and rewards ongoing employee input, which only makes sense. The employees are on the front lines of what is going on in the organization, and can provide valuable feedback to continually improve the Ritz experience. The hotel also encourages and provides opportunity for employees to advance in the organization. With this kind of buy-in, one can see why they have attained an esteemed status.

GROWTH DESPITE ECONOMIC DOWNTURN

Since September 11, 2001, there has been an obvious economic downturn, international conflict, reduction in travel and mounting hotel vacancies. And how has the Ritz fared? According to Van Grinsven: "During the last five years, while other major hotels were trying to maintain the status quo, we opened thirty new hotels, nearly doubling our size." He went on to say the only challenge with such growth was making sure all new staff were prepared to deliver the Ritz experience with excellence.

LEADERSHIP

The Ritz-Carlton service model is so esteemed it warranted the creation of The Ritz-Carlton Leadership Center in 1999. The center offers training that has saturated business leaders from 175 companies with the Ritz-Carlton service model. One statistic that might help you understand why they have achieved such high regard for their service model, besides the awards they have won, (according to the Ritz) is that 51% of the hotel's guests are repeat patrons. Their system works worldwide in thirteen countries using sixty-six languages.

The Gold Standard is the foundation for their philosophy and values, and it has five parts:

The Credo, The Motto, The Three Steps of Service, The Basics, and The Employee Promise.

I'll go into it briefly, but this information is available on the Ritz-Carlton website should you want to explore it further.

THE CREDO

The Ritz-Carlton Hotel is a place where the genuine care and comfort of our guests is our highest mission.

We pledge to provide the finest personal service and facilities for our guests who will always enjoy a warm, relaxed, yet refined ambience.

The Ritz-Carlton experience enlivens the senses, instills well being, and fulfills even the unexpressed wishes and needs of our guests.

THE MOTTO

At the Ritz-Carlton, L.L.C., "We are ladies and gentlemen serving ladies and gentlemen." This motto exemplifies the anticipatory service provided by all staff members.

Three Steps Of Service
1. A warm and sincere greeting. Use the guest name, if and when possible.
2. Anticipation and compliance with guest needs.
3. Fond farewell. Give them a warm good-bye and use their names, if and when possible.

THE 20 BASICS

1. The credo is the principal belief of our company. It must be known, and energized by all.
2. Our Motto is "We are ladies and gentlemen serving ladies and gentleman." As service professionals we treat our guests and each other with respect and dignity.
3. The Three Steps of Service are the foundation of Ritz-Carlton hospitality. These steps must be used in every interaction to ensure satisfaction, retention and loyalty.
4. The Employee Promise is the basis for our Ritz-Carlton work environment. It will be honored by all employees.

5. All employees will successfully complete annual Training Cert-ification for their position.
6. Company objectives are communicated to all employees. It is everyone's responsibility to support them.
7. To create pride and joy in the workplace, all employees have the right to be involved in the planning of work that affects them.
8. Each employee will continuously identify defects throughout the hotel.
9. It is the responsibility of each employee to create a work environ-ment of teamwork and lateral service so that the needs of our guests and each other are met.
10. Each employee is empowered. For example, when a guest has a problem or needs something special, you should break away from your regular duties, address and resolve the issue.
11. Uncompromising levels of cleanliness are the responsibility of every employee.
12. To provide the finest personal service for our guests, each employee should identify and record individual guest preferences.
13. Never lose a guest. Instant guest pacification is the responsibility of each employee. Whoever records a complaint will own it, resolve it to the guest's satisfaction and record it.
14. "Smile, we are on stage." Always maintain positive eye contact. Use the proper vocabulary with our guest. (Use words like "Good Morning," "Certainly," "I'll be happy to," and "My Pleasure.")
15. Be an ambassador of your Hotel in and outside of your work place. Always talk positively. Communicate any concerns to the appropriate person.
16. Escort guests rather than pointing out directions to another area of the hotel.
17. Use Ritz-Carlton phone etiquette. Answer within three rings and with a "smile." Use the guest name when possible. When necessary, ask the caller "may I place you on hold?" Do not screen calls and eliminate call transfers when possible. Adhere to voice mail standards.

18. Take pride in and care of your personal appearance. Everyone is responsible for conveying a professional image by adhering to the Ritz-Carlton clothing and grooming standards.
19. Think safety first. Each employee is responsible for creating a safe, secure and accident free environment for all guests and each other. Be aware of all fire and emergency procedures and report security risks immediately.
20. Protecting the assets of a Ritz-Carlton is the responsibility of every employee. Conserve energy and properly maintain our hotels and protect the environment.

THE EMPLOYEE PROMISE

1. At the Ritz-Carlton, our ladies and gentlemen are the most important resource in our service commitment to our guests.
2. By applying the principles of trust, honesty, respect, integrity and commitment, we nurture and maximize our talent to the benefit of each individual and the company.
3. The Ritz-Carlton fosters a work environment where diversity is valued, quality of life is enhanced, individual aspirations are fulfilled, and The Ritz-Carlton mystique is strengthened.
4. The Ritz-Carlton mission is to provide the finest personal service and facilities throughout the world. The atmosphere is warm and relaxed and the ambience embraces the uniqueness of the local culture. The variety of services offered will enable you to create your own experience.

Cesar Ritz would be proud that today phrases like "puttin' on the Ritz" and "Ritzy" can be traced back to the vision he had for the company in 1898. Cesar would also be pleased that the "ladies and gentlemen" of the Ritz-Carlton today continue to create the royal experience that he envisioned, and now we have come to expect from the Ritz-Carlton.

The ten attributes of advocate marketing and how the Ritz addresses each:

- **Differentiating Factor**: "The royal treatment," "the way the hotel embraces the culture they are in," "the ladies and gentlemen."
- **Customer loyalty**: A reported "51% of the hotels guests are repeat patrons." On average during their lifetime, the patrons of the Ritz spend $250,000.
- **Saving the customer time**: Step # 9 of the twenty basics: "To provide the finest personal services for our guests each employee is responsible for identifying and recording individual guest preferences." Now this may not seem like a huge time saving ordeal but to an establishment that caters to the relatively wealthy, this is very important. If successful, busy people actually make it to a vacation destination, they don't want to waste their valuable time describing and re-describing what it is that they want. Their time is maximized, because the way they want to be treated, the special requests that they would spend time describing to the employee at the Ritz can all be avoided, because there is a permanent record of what that particular customer wants.
- **Customer "experience" so a "story" is told about the company**: Besides staying in a Ritz yourself so you have your own story, call someone you know who has stayed at one. You will find the stories captivating and desirable so that you'll be compelled to plan a Ritz-Carlton experience as soon as possible.
- **Create customization in your product or service**: "#12 of the 20 Basics "To provide the finest personal service for our guests, each employee is responsible for identifying and recording individual guest preferences."
- **Employees feel a part of the company**: The Ritz employees have "the lowest turnover rate in the hotel industry." Opportunities for advancement within the organization as well as investment dollars towards advanced college degrees. Each employee is empowered to allocate $2,000 towards immediate resolution for the customer.
- **The forgiveness factor**: The only thing I have to say here is that:

employees are empowered to resolve situations directly with customers, "up to $2,000 per incident without the prior approval of a supervisor." Because of this a situation where the Ritz-Carlton would have to ask for forgiveness from a mistake not immediately resolved, would be rare indeed.

- **Is the customer willing to pay a premium**: While the average hotel stay at Half Moon Bay, California is about $134, the Ritz-Carlton Half Moon Bay is $345 per night (Fall 2005). That is a 157% difference in price for a room to sleep in. In Dearborn, Michigan an average night stay is roughly $90 per night and the Ritz-Carlton in Dearborn by contrast is $259 per night (Fall 2005), which is a 187% mark up between the average hotel stay in the area and a night at the Ritz.

- **Does the competition try and emulate products or features of this company**: The Boston Ritz-Carlton introduced room and service standards unprecedented in America that are now considered basic for today's luxury hotels. Private baths, elevated black tie dress code, smaller intimate lobbies. The phrases that have been coined by the Ritz-Carlton, "ritzy," and "puttin' on the ritz."

- **Don't think big, think small**: Employees not being allowed to point is a small policy the Ritz has implemented, but being "escorted" to wherever it is you would love to go at the Ritz, is what causes one to feel like royalty during your stay. Allowing employees the empowerment to immediately "fix" a customer complaint. The "authority to allocate up to $2,000 of resources for solving a customer's complaint immediately, without a supervisor's approval" is small compared to the fact that this institution has a built in forgiveness factor because of this policy.

Lastly, the policy of addressing the customer by name whenever possible is another small employee policy with the "feeling of royalty ramifications."

Notes:

_____

_____

_____

_____

_____

_____

_____

_____

_____

_____

_____

_____

_____

_____

_____

_____

_____

_____

_____

CHAPTER SIX

A TIRE, A ROOF
AND A PACKAGE

"I know of no other fortitude than stubbornness in the face of overwhelming odds."

— **Louis Nizer**
English lawyer famous for his quotes (1900's)

"In playing ball, or in life, a person occasionally gets the opportunity to do something great. When that time comes, only two things matter: being prepared to seize the moment and having courage to take your best swing."

— **Hank Aaron**
Known as one of the all time home run leaders in baseball, with 755 home runs during his career (1960's-1970's)

So what do a service station, a roofing company and a courier service have in common? We've explored large companies that are above their competition for the advocate marketing they create. But if you have a much smaller company, or you are a manager, you might need to relate to these qualities on a much smaller scale. So let's look at three different and much smaller companies and see how they reconfirm the ten qualities that create advocate marketing.

So what do these three companies have in common? Besides all having the ten essentials for advocate marketing and operating in the Dallas Fort Worth area, they all operate 24 hours a day, seven days a week 365 days a year. They all have low turnover, even though each of their industries have typically high turnover. Additionally, they all have their employees wear "uniforms," which is very unusual in all of their respective industries. The annual sales of these three companies range from 2.5 million per year to 21 million.

Certainly after sharing their numbers, I have established in your mind that they are all in their own right successful. I'd like to share with you their stories and how they have more than their success in common. I chose these three companies because I know the owners and respect them for the successful businesses they have built.

A TIRE

I'll start with Sam. Got a flat tire and it's 2 a.m.? If you live in Fort Worth, Texas, no problem; you call Sam. Sam's operation is "open" 24 hours a day, seven days a week, 365 days a year.

I don't know where you live, but if you get ready to head to the airport for an early flight and you notice that you have a flat tire, whom do you call for help? Many people would not have someone to get them out of a jam like that. But I don't have to worry, because I have Sam and his company, Fort Worth Tire.

The situation I just described happened to me a few years ago, and thanks to Sam I made my flight. Of course, Sam doesn't make much of the calls anymore, but someone from his shop does. And just as when Sam used to come himself, when his employee leaves, I feel taken care of.

Now I don't know about you, but having come from a very small town (population 3,000), the experiences I have had with Fort Worth Tire makes me feel as if Fort Worth Texas (population 603,000, 2004) is a small town. I have heard others comment on how Fort Worth "feels" like a small town. I call it the biggest small town you'll ever experience. I think companies like Fort Worth Tire are one of the reasons why.

Just like in my hometown, business was done with a handshake, and you knew and trusted whoever was servicing your car. Most likely you'd see each other at church on Sunday, so it wasn't like you could get away with treating your customers badly, since you would frequently see them around town. As I continue to describe to you the experiences of Fort Worth Tire, you will understand the small town feeling that you receive when you do business with them.

Since the airport incident I described, Sam and his company have saved me at least three other times. The last time was recently when I was meeting for breakfast with a consultant for this book. Now, I hadn't needed to call for a couple years, so I really hoped that when I called my experience would be exactly as I had remembered.

I had just bought this car and it had new tires on it, but when I left my meeting to head to the office, I noticed I had a flat. With a full day of meetings, I really didn't have time to be inconvenienced with the worry of getting my tire fixed. I called the number I had for Sam at Fort Worth Tire, and hoped he would come through again. Even though I wasn't far away, I knew that I probably wasn't his only call today, and didn't know how long I would have to wait.

Within fifteen minutes, Sam showed up to see if he could fix my tire there on the spot. When I think back, about half of the time he or his employee were able to fix the tire right where the car was sitting. Otherwise, the repair needed had to be done at the shop so my car was towed in, and I was given a ride to my office. Either way, any of these times could have been an awful "ruin your day" experience, but thanks to Sam and his team, my days didn't turn out bad at all. It always made me feel like I was taken care of; like I had an old friend to call when I was in a jam.

Yes, I know I have a spare in my car, and I'm sure there is a tool back there that would enable me to get my old tire off and the new one on but sorry, I'm just not doing it. There are just some things that it makes more sense to pay someone else to do. Not to mention, most of the times I needed Sam I was in a business suit. He certainly saved me time, not to mention the aggravation, headache or the worry of one more thing to deal with during the day.

PEACE OF MIND

How much does that kind of peace of mind cost these days? Well, in Fort Worth, if you call Sam, fifty dollars for the house call. Of course, it could be more depending on what needs to be done.

Sam is very honest. Twice now I have needed a new tire when I have had a flat. Both times, Sam told me the price of the exact model of tire I would be replacing. And then he did something that I have to say I can't imagine many small business owners doing. He looked up the price of a comparable tire, that he felt, was just as good as the name brand tires I was trying to replace, and he gave me a choice as to which one I wanted. He is in the tire business, so if he tells me it is just as good a tire without the brand name, I'm inclined to believe him.

This last time, his helpfulness saved me $100 and the time I had to replace all four, it was $400. If that fifty dollar house call was say, one hundred dollars, it would still be worth it for the feeling of being taken care of and his honest insight, that has saved me money more than once.

THE TOUR

When I selected businesses that I felt were above the average in customer service, or that I knew something unique about, I decided to go back to each of their offices with a fresh eye to see what made them tick, keeping the ten qualities in mind.

As I walked into Sam's service station, I noticed things a little differently. First, I am very fond of gas/service stations. My grandfather Mason, one of the most favorite people in my life, had made his livelihood from running a gas and service station. As a child, I would spend most of the summer there "working" in the service station, helping out. I'm sure looking back I was more in the way, but he never let on to that, he just acted like I was meant to be there as much as anyone else.

Like most service stations, including his and Sam's, you can smell oil and gas when you walk in. The coffee pot, not the cleanest you have ever seen, is there for you to help yourself to a cup. The entry way has a few seats in it and some magazines to browse, which is typical. What gets your attention is that as soon as you walk in, someone says, "How can we help you today." They make you feel like you are the most important customer that has walked in and whatever problem you are having, is now their problem. They are going to come up with a way to fix it, and offer to give you a ride to wherever you want, while your "problem" is being fixed.

DOESN'T TAKE ALL OF THE CREDIT

When I interviewed Sam in his office, he insisted that his partner, Brad "Bear" Wright and his office manager, Shelly Leggett sit in on our interview. Right away, that told me something about Sam; he didn't want all of the credit for the success of his shop. To him it was a team effort, and he knew that his success had as much to do with the quality of his team, as it did with him.

As I waited for everyone to get their morning coffee, I noticed the walls of the office were lined with personal hand-written thank you notes and photos of staff and customers.

Sam described for me how he got started in the tire business, in January of 1979.

He had worked for a tire company (no longer in business) and he brought with him the little brother he never had, "Bear" Wright. "Bear" and Sam left this company after a few years and went to another local tire company. After seeing the unethical way they did business, "Bear" and Sam decided to venture out on their own with their own service shop. Since most of the customers from this place really came there because of "Bear" and Sam, they were fortunate to start out with a good customer base from the loyalty they had built at these previous stations.

I picked up a few other interesting tidbits during the interview. One is that everyday "Bear" reads the obituaries in the paper to make sure that if any of their customers pass away, they don't go unnoticed. As a result, Fort Worth Tire spends an average of $5,000 on floral arrangements every year.

Every year for the last eighteen years, Fort Worth Tire has had a huge Christmas party attended by from 1,200 to 1,800 customers. Sam goes all out on the party, where no invitations are sent, by the way, because everyone knows it is the first Friday in December every year, and starts right after work. The party has huge outdoor tents with heaters to keep warm, and the theme is the same with black jack, craps and most other casino games complete with professional dealers Sam pays to make the party authentic for the customers.

During the interview, Sam invited a customer from the lobby, Mr. McClain, to join us. You see Mr. McClain, Sam went on to tell me, was a thirty-year customer of his and Bear's, and he told a story that relates to the "customer experience" and the "forgiveness factor" attributes. Mr. McClain stated that he continues to come to Fort Worth Tire and encourages his friends and family to go as well, because he knows that they will "make good on what they might do wrong."

He went on to state that if they made a mistake, which they had in Mr. McClain's case, he knew they would make it right. He also said that he wouldn't feel comfortable recommending them if he didn't believe in them himself. He recalled the "mistake" that was a few years ago and was a simple tire rebalancing job that was done by Fort Worth Tire. Mr. McClain stated that when he drove the car, it just didn't feel right. He brought the car back to Fort Worth Tire; they gladly rebalanced the tires and did not charge him for redoing this service.

"THEY CARE ABOUT ME HERE"

The other employee present in the interview, Shelly, emphasized that she has had three different jobs over the last sixteen years, the last job working for a bank, and she has never felt a part of a company before her job at Fort Worth Tire. Although she has only been at the company for a little over a year, she already feels like part of the Fort Worth Tire family. She feels they care about her, value what she does, and listen to the ideas and input that she has to offer (these are two of the three aspects from the Gallup study of what ranks as most important regardless of pay, to corporate executives). Speaking of pay, Shelly took a good-sized pay cut to come to Fort Worth Tire, but she said, "It was worth it."

One more item on creating a positive experience for employees and helping them feel a part of the company, Sam has taken many employees on vacation trips for fun and picked up the entire tab. One very memorable year was when he took eighteen employees and twelve customers to Las Vegas for Super Bowl weekend and footed the bill for the entire trip.

THROWING A PEBBLE INTO THE WATER

The following comment made by Sam caused me to think of the Gallup study that talked about the cascading effect of negative management creating negative employees. But of course, in Fort Worth Tire's case, the cascading effect is positive, where positive management creates positive employees, who in turn treat the customer in a positive manner.

When I asked Sam if he had any final comments on customer service, he said he saw what he did for his customers like throwing a pebble into the water and watching the rings that ricochet out from where the pebble is dropped. "That is like our business, and there is no reason the ripple affect won't continue as long as we continue to give superb treatment (service) to our customers, they will in turn tell others about us and the business will never stop."

Fort Worth Tire and the ten attributes:
Differentiating factor: Honesty and the ability to take care of whatever the customer may need. For example, if the customer needs a service that Fort Worth Tire doesn't provide, they will take the customer's car

to an appropriate car service company in their network and then bring it back to Fort Worth Tire for the customer to pick up there.

Customer loyalty:
Fort Worth Tire sponsors softball teams that many customers play in and employees often play with customers.

Most employees know and address customers by name. Some of the customers have known Sam and "Bear" since 1967, and are friends from junior high and high school. Sam stated that there isn't a day that goes by that at least one person comes in whom they've known for 30 years and some days as many as six people will come by who fit that criteria.

Saving the customer time:
Fort Worth Tires takes the customer to work while their tire is being worked on. They also take the car to another car service place, to do extra work on the car that Fort Worth Tire doesn't do to avoid the time that the extra step would cost the customer. Call in towing for a car if necessary so the customer doesn't have to. They know the customer just wants to get back on the road with a repaired car or tire as quickly and as inexpensively as possible.

Customer experience:
The friendly atmosphere when you enter and are offered, "How can we help you today?" Being introduced by name as often as not. The listening to what the customer wants and the feeling of being taken care of no matter what the situation is and Fort Worth Tire, making your problem their problem until it is resolved.

Product or service customized or personalized:
Giving the customer the option of name brand products or generic, depending on the customer's budget. Or giving the customer a spare tire to "get by" for a few months until they can afford to replace their tires. Fort Worth Tire will offer to give the customer the tire and trust

them to come back when they can afford to pay for a new one. Also, depending on what kind of driving will be done by the customer, Fort Worth Tire will recommend the specific tire that makes sense for their specific situation.

Employees feel apart of the company:
Employees comment on witnessing Sam and Bear chipping in to help answer the phone, sweep, and fix a tire etc. They aren't too good to do any job that they ask employees to do which causes employees to want to work hard for the company.

Employees feel that Fort Worth Tire truly cares about them and rewards them with vacation trips and also listens to employee's feedback with an open door policy to whoever has a suggestion, no matter what position they hold at Fort Worth Tire.

Forgiveness factor:
Customer Mr. McClain described a time when Fort Worth Tire rebalanced a tire and when it didn't feel right when he drove it, he brought it back and Fort Worth Tire rebalanced the tire at no charge. Customers like Mr. McClain know that they will make good on what they might do wrong so are willing to look past mistakes from time to time.

Customer willing to pay a premium:
Yes, Fort Worth tire knows they are not the least expensive tire service company and aren't going to be as inexpensive as a comparable chain store. But they try to make that up by giving more than expected service so that the extra cost is worth it to the customer.

Has the competition tried to emulate an aspect of your business?
Yes, a larger brand name tire company started providing 24 hour 7 days a week, 365 days of the year service after Fort Worth Tire implemented this benefit. The larger brand name, however only wants the larger trucking business, so Fort Worth Tire has a niche in

being able and willing to provide this "open all year round" service to customers large and small.

Don't think big think small:
Wearing uniforms so other's see you as a "professional" in an industry that is rarely respected. Letting the customer borrow a good used tire to get by while they can come up with the funds to buy a new tire.

A ROOF

I'm sure you have been around successful people and you have an impression of how a successful person acts. I notice an aura about them, the way they handle themselves, and their confident walk. That was my first impression of the owners of Empire Roofing. When I met Ronnie and Sandra McGlothlin, owners of Empire Roofing, several years ago, I could tell they were successful.

I am fascinated by the psychology of people and what makes people tick. Furthermore, what makes them successful, especially when they have overwhelming odds.

MILLIONAIRE NEXT DOOR

Dr. Thomas Stanley, who wrote the best selling book *The Millionaire Next Door*, also wrote *The Millionaire Woman Next Door*, and he could have easily put Ronnie and Sandra McGlothlin in his books. There are certain qualifications that Dr. Stanley used when he sought out and interviewed these millionaires for his books. For starters, they had to be self-made. No business could be handed down by another generation to them, and like the title states, they had to have at least a one million dollar net worth.

When I do speaking engagements, I discuss both of these books. Many people may think that the only way to create wealth is through the lottery, gambling, inheritance or being one of the "lucky" people in life. In Dr. Stanley's books you learn that even though there were some that would be considered lucky, or some that did receive inheritances, the bulk of their wealth came from good old-fashioned, work to earn the money, and good old-fashioned discipline with their money to keep more of what they do make. Like Hank Aaron states, these people prepared themselves for success and then came out swinging.

Not only were they not given their wealth, but also their spending habits are not what you might expect. The concept of the millionaire next door is that you can't tell they are the millionaire next door. According to Dr. Stanley's research, few own high-end luxury cars, few are members of country clubs, and they don't necessarily shop where you might expect, or buy what you might expect them to buy. In my presentations, I ask the audience what they think the number one credit card is for men. I have never in over 50 presentations gotten the correct guess. According to Dr. Stanley's research, it is Sears. And the preferred car of those millionaire men, according to Stanley is the Ford F150.

In his other book where he interviewed women with the same "millionaire next door criteria," I was impressed with the stories. If you did nothing else but read the stories of how these women got started, you would undoubtedly be inspired. One story that sticks in my mind is one of a woman who got her start by running away from home because of fear for her life at sixteen. She now is about fifty, with a five million dollar net worth. She started as a waitress and now is a successful restaurateur in her own home town. The one thing that struck Dr. Stanley when he interviewed these women was that they did not dwell on their past misfortune or mistakes.

When we work with people, helping them do the things they need to do, our humanness causes us to beat ourselves up for our past mistakes or to make excuses for why we aren't where we want to be. If there is one thing to learn from these women, it is we would all do ourselves a favor to move on and forget our past as soon as possible. Learn from our mistakes if we need to and don't make excuses.

ACCEPT NO EXCUSES

Now, when you meet the McGlothlin's you can tell right away, they accept no excuses for themselves or their employees to not be the most successful roofing company that they can be.

Ronnie and Sandra started their roofing business out of their garage, because of their desire to "be their own boss." Ronnie had the hands-on experience in roofing and knew the skills and what had to be done to do quality work. Sandra had the financial sense and marketing sense that was needed to get the business started. Sandra laughs when she talks about the timing of starting their business, "With two toddlers to take care of, what could possibly be a better time to start your own business?"

It reminded me of how through our life, when does it ever seem to be the best time to do anything? Go on a vacation, start a business, start planning your financial future. But just like the people in Dr. Stanley's book, no excuses; just do it.

What started out as a way to pay the bills has now become, "The roofing company by which all others are measured." That motto hangs on the wall at Empire, and was given to the company by a safety consultant that Empire had hired ten years previously to evaluate Empire's safety. It has become the tag line for the business, and is proudly displayed on the company uniforms.

RECOGNIZING A NEW BUSINESS OPPORTUNITY

Empire Roofing is a commercial re-roofing company. They do not do new roofs but replace existing roofs and only on commercial properties. Because of this, they have a large need for roll-off dumpsters. As the workers tear down the old roofs, they need dumpsters to throw the old material into and be able to transport it off of the property.

On an average size job for Empire, there could be twenty workers on a crew tearing off the old roof. Twenty people can take off a large amount of a roof in a short time. This caused a problem, because each job needed from five to sixty-eight dumpsters to complete a roof. The dumpster supplier Empire used would always drop off the standard two or three dumpsters for each job, which wasn't enough to handle all of the material. When Empire would call and request more, there would always be a day or so delay and even then Empire was only given a few more dumpsters to use. This caused the workers to need to throw the material on the ground and then go back to the site a few days later when more dumpsters arrived, and "handle" the same material again. This was very inefficient and time consuming and what inspired the McGlothlin's to start their second business of providing roll-off dumpsters to keep up with their own demand.

Ironically, the biggest customers in this roll-off dumpster business is other roofing contractors. They understand the needs of the contractors since they are one, and ask these roofing companies how many dumpsters are needed for a job. The customer then decides how many dumpsters they need dropped off at each job site. Now that's customized service.

CUSTOMER RELATIONSHIPS

When I asked if there were any other comments related to customer service that they would like to make, Sandra stated that their success had to do with the relationships that they have built with their customers.

Most of their customers know Ronnie and Sandra from their years in business or from their positions on boards and associations in the roofing industry. But they will often physically take their foreman, supervisor and roofer to the job site to introduce them to the owner or manager of the property they will be working on. They introduce them as the person who will be handling their account so they have a face-to-face meeting to meet them, and so they can be comfortable with who will be doing the work on their property.

When you walk into Empire roofing's lobby, you notice instantly that this is a professional organization. The lobby could be a doctor's office, a CPA's or an attorney's office for that matter. You wouldn't know it was a roofing company until you start to look at the photos in the lobby of the many projects that Empire has done, and the many awards they have won for them.

You don't get what you would expect from a roofing company when you walk into their meeting room. It is a cross between a boardroom and a typical meeting room of a small business. What lines the walls of the meeting room are eye-catching positive phrases on teamwork, discipline, a positive attitude and exemplary customer service. Just by visiting the company, you get the feeling that this is no ordinary business, but a first class operation in an industry with little respect. And if you had the opportunity to meet Ronnie or Sandra, you'd get the feeling that they don't have or accept many excuses for not being successful.

Empire Roofing and the ten attributes:
Differentiating factor:
The quality in everything we do, putting out a quality product, and being known like UPS, the cleanest company in our industry. The customer doesn't expect cleanliness in the roofing business or expect the workers to wear uniforms, but Empire roofing does and the equipment, trucks they drive, etc. are kept as clean as possible.

Empire uses higher quality material than expected from their customer so the roof is more durable, lasting longer and not needing replacement as often as when cheaper quality material is used. Empire shows how by using the higher quality material the roof will last for example five years longer and when that is factored in the extra cost is minimal to doing it right the first time.

Customer loyalty:
Develop a relationship with the customer, know them and their property as well as their family. Because of the loyalty and trust Empire has built over the years, they can work with the property owners' tenant so the property owner doesn't have to. Work one on one with the property owner showing them where the problem in the roof is and what the fix is for their problem.

Saving the customer time:
Empire will often have lunch brought in to explain the needed repairs for the roof being worked on. All roofers have digital cameras, so the property owner doesn't have to climb on the roof to view the needed repair, or even be in town for that matter. The owner can have digital photos sent to them with the repair estimate and can email approval of work to be done or contact Empire with questions based on the photo and estimate.

Customer experience:
The quick response time and 24 hour 7 days a week, 365 days of the year ability to patch a roof immediately. This insures expensive artwork or computer circuits won't be damaged by water, while the estimate is done by Empire to determine what repairs are needed.

Product or service customized or personalized:
Empire has introduced a time saving and customizing feature called E Leak. With this service a leak can be reported and emailed to Empire. On their website is a form to fill out, email or fax in for this request. This avoids the break down in communication that often happens when the receptionist takes the details over the phone. Through E Leak, the customer can let Empire know the urgency of the request and what is possibly going to be damaged by the leak. Empire allows the customer to tell them how many roll off containers they need. Many disposal container companies only drop off a certain number for every job, regardless if potentially more are needed.

Employees feel apart of the company:
At Empire, the foreman has the power to hire and fire their own men. As a result, foremen often hire friends and family. And the foreman knows the kind of worker they need for their jobs. Every quarter each team is given a $100 per man safety bonus if no injuries have been reported for that quarter. If there is an accident and it is determined it could have been prevented by the team, then the whole crew doesn't

get this $100 per man bonus. This helps the employees take care of each other and since Empire implemented this benefit, fraudulent accident claims are almost non-existent. At every employee's ten year anniversary, a Rolex watch is given. Empire has 150 employees and 30 of them have watches, with another 10 to be given out in 2005.

Forgiveness factor:
At Empire, when a mistake is made, they are quick to admit the error and then make a proposal on how to fix it. They even ask the customer if the resolution is acceptable or not. Empire keeps the customer in the loop and tells them what measures they have implemented to try and insure that the same error doesn't happen again.

Customer willing to pay a premium:
Yes, the customer knows that for the prompt response to protect valuable items on the property, it is worth every extra penny they might spend on a roof. Also, companies like Bank of America, Phillip Morris and Kroger want qualified roofing contractors for their property and know that the cost will be more to have a qualified roofer do their work. Empire is also "certified" for warranty approved contractors, which gives peace of mind to many of their larger customers.

Has the competition tried to emulate an aspect of your business:
Ten years ago, Empire hired a safety consultant to critique them on their safety standards. After their review he gave them a plaque that read "The roofing company by which all others are measured." This phrase is now on Empire's uniforms. Additionally, Empire has an open door policy when it comes to competitors wanting to witness first hand what Empire does. When I asked, "Why would you share your business with your competition?" The response was: "Good competition is always better than bad competition."

Don't think big think small:
The convenience of E Leak so customers can let Empire know about

their problem on their time, when it is convenient for them.

A PACKAGE

Much like the owners of the previous two companies, the owners of the courier service saw a need for the business they started. The business owners, Tammy Patterson and Lena Flores, had both started at entry levels at the same bank. The bank at the time used courier services for their package pick up and deposit bag deliveries. They witnessed the couriers coming into the bank lobby in shabby clothes, torn jeans and t-shirts, and it occurred to them how bad the appearance was, especially in a bank or a place of business.

GOOD FIRST IMPRESSION

Like it or not, we are to some extent judged by our appearance and our first impression. When an employee is handling important shipments for a bank and walking through the bank lobby, the shabby appearance is important. Words like "trustworthy," "honest," and "dependable," just don't come to mind when you have holes in your jeans or have on a ratty t-shirt.

After receiving this feedback repeatedly, Tammy and Lena went to the bank with their idea. Wouldn't they prefer a courier service that would have clean-cut drivers dressed professionally and more "business looking," serving their bank? The bank was impressed and liked the idea. So in 1984, with a $5,000 line of credit, and $500 initial capital investment from the two partners, CitySprint 1-800-DELIVER (formally Striders Courier, Inc.) was born. By the way, the bank Tammy and Lena worked at when they got their idea is still a customer.

NICHE MARKET

CitySprint 1-800-DELIVER now extends its professional services to include a market niche of medical services such as lab, blood work

A TIRE, A ROOF AND A PACKAGE

and various specimens. Because of their fairly new niche in the medical industry, they now provide OSHA training for their drivers. They utilize coolers for their bio-hazard medical deliveries. This is obviously a very critical product to deliver, with individual's lives and health depending on the timely and non-perished delivery of specimens.

ON TIME OR ON US

In addition to the professional appearance of its drivers, CitySprint 1-800-DELIVER also puts their money where their mouth is when it comes to their on-time delivery. Several years ago, CitySprint implemented a guarantee that is now being copied by other courier services: if it is not on time, it is free. In fact their tag line is: "On time or it's on us."

If CitySprint drops the ball, they will pick up the cost.

I have had personal experiences with this company for business. When I can't risk the untimely delivery of paperwork needed for one of our clients, I call CitySprint 1-800-DELIVER. After our staff makes the request, in our mind, the business is done. Our staff spends literally 30% of their time, verifying that a task that was to be completed, actually gets completed so we can be assured our clients requests are taken care of.

The peace of mind that comes with knowing a task will be seen through to completion, without needing to spend time verifying it, is refreshing indeed.

METICULOUS RECORDS

Another benefit to customers doing business with CitySprint 1-800-DELIVER is they keep meticulous records, and according to their records, they have 94% on-time performance. The company also keeps detailed records in their database of all pick ups and deliveries. If a customer needs to research any of the business they have done with CitySprint, everything is recorded and can be given to any customer upon request or by looking online.

This saves businesses time as they don't have to research for themselves this information, or even try to keep track of it. CitySprint has got it covered for them. And at the end of the year as a CitySprint customer, for your bookkeeping purposes, you can request an itemized record of all the jobs from the past year or view it online.

Another time saving feature is the ability to request deliveries or pick ups via the internet. This is helpful for CitySprint as well as the customer. When emailing a request, an employee can multitask by answering the phone for example at the same time they are requesting a delivery. It helps CitySprint by having a written record of the requested job. This is more efficient as the request can then be sent to a driver electronically. To the client, this is a seamless process, and, like our other two companies, there is someone on call at all times. So, in effect, CitySprint is open for its customer's convenience, 24 hours a day 7 days a week, 365 days a year.

OUR PEOPLE

The owners of CitySprint had these final comments: "The one thing that will make or break us is our people." To insure that the contracted drivers at CitySprint feel included and apart of the operation, every day the daily production report is shared with each driver. The production report tells the driver exactly how much CitySprint charges each customer on the driver's route each day, how much they paid the driver for the service, thus showing the driver CitySprint's net profit from that business.

Being open, honest and willing to share this kind of information builds loyalty with their contractors. Tammy added: "When we hire our drivers, we tell them they are independent contractors with no benefits, but that we (CitySprint) are partnering in this together."

CitySprint 1-800-DELIVER and the ten attributes:
Differentiating feature:
The quality of their drivers, their professional appearance and

uniforms they wear. The cutting edge technology that CitySprint uses to keep up with business and deliver products with the ability to track packages and orders via the internet. The dispatcher assigns a job to the driver and the driver can respond instantaneously. CitySprint uses Nextel software that provides two way data device that allows voice response. This allows a seamless transfer of information to the customers while maintaining safety for the driver. CitySprint is "open" 24/7 365 days a year.

Customer Loyalty:
CitySprint creates loyalty by building relationships and giving good quality consistent contact, staying in touch with customers throughout the year through correspondence every few months and letting them know that CitySprint appreciates their business. CitySprint gets more new business from existing customers than any other marketing or advertisment services.

Saving the Customer Time:
Orders can be placed on the internet so someone at an office can answer the phone while placing a pick up order at the same time. Multi-tasking for the assistant or receptionist saves time. Error free delivery and pick up, saves the customer time because they are confident and don't have to worry or double check on package delivery or pick up. CitySprint also stores all pick ups and deliveries so that if a customer wants a history of past deliveries, CitySprint can pull the records, saving them time from needing to pull their own records for the information.

Customer "Experience:"
The story for CitySprint would be the time saving experience the customer receives because of the ability to use the internet for ordering so someone at an office can answer the phone, while placing a pick up order at the same time. This allows multi-tasking for the assistant or receptionist, saving them time. Also being able to pull records of historical data so the

customer doesn't have to worry about keeping that data or searching for it. They know CitySprint can retrieve the information at any time. The guarantee of "On time or it's on us." This "error free" delivery saves the customer time because they are more confident and don't have to worry or double check on package delivery or pick up.

Product or Service Customized or Personalized:
If a customer requests that they have the same driver, then that driver is given to them for delivery and pick up. Many banks like this feature because of the security of knowing the driver and trusting the specific driver with their deposit bags. Banks also may need to give the driver keys to the lock box at the bank if the delivery is after banking hours. Often CitySprint will take the drivers out to meet the prospective customer so that they can get to know the driver that will be handling their pick up and deliveries. CitySprint has also started OSHA training for their drivers since they have been handling bio hazardous material for the medical industry.

One of the company's clients, the YMCA, is very sensitive to background checks of employees, since these drivers will often be around children for their jobs. CitySprint does background and criminal checks on all drivers working with them and the YMCA can feel secure as a result. This is a service that many couriers don't take the extra step to do with their drivers.

Employees feel a part of the Company:
Each day CitySprint produces a report called the daily production report. This report is openly shared with the drivers, so they can see the profit and loss for the day from the work that they have participated in. The owners of CitySprint feel that this honesty and willingness to share this kind of information builds loyalty in their drivers. CitySprint's drivers are independent contractors with no benefits. CitySprint explains to the drivers when they sign on to work with CitySprint that they are "partnering in this together."

All employees as well as contractors receive a 3% commission on business they refer to CitySprint, and that commission continues to that employee/contractor as long as they are working with CitySprint. CitySprint keeps meticulous records of business as well as drivers' history; as a result they can calculate that 47% of their contractors have been with them 2 years or longer. This is way over the industry average.

Forgiveness Factor:
One of the owners of CitySprint recalled losing a bank delivery bag with thousands of checks in it. CitySprint's insurance paid all but $25,000 of the missing checks. CitySprint decided to use some of its business capital to make up the $25,000 difference. This is something they didn't "have" to do but felt to keep credibility with this bank customer they needed to. They also went on to keep the customer in the loop as to what systems were put in place to prevent the incident from happening again.

One of the reasons CitySprint feels they continue to get asked for the business is they are open and honest when there is a mistake. They also include the customer on the resolution of the error and then what is changed to insure it doesn't happen again.

Customer Willing to pay a premium?
Yes, they pay more for the consistent, quality service that CitySprint provides. The customer also knows that this company has a "On time or it's on us" policy. So they know that CitySprint is accountable for timely delivery and pick ups and they put their money where their mouth is with the guarantee they offer all customers.

Has the competition tried to emulate an aspect of your business?
Other couriers in the DFW area did not start offering the "On time or it's on us" policy until after CitySprint implemented this service. Some have even gone as far as copying their slogan: "On time or it's on us."

Don't think big, think small:
Wearing uniforms so other's see you as a "professional" in an industry that is rarely respected. Introducing customers to "their driver" and letting them take part in the selection of their driver, if possible.

STRIKING SIMILARITIES

The similarities that all three of these businesses have with one another are quite interesting. And remember, when I was contemplating small businesses to interview, the only thing I knew they had in common was that they were all located in the Dallas Fort Worth area, they were successful, and I happened to know each of the owners. Yet you can see that all three companies have something else in common: they take their business and their customer service seriously.

You can tell from the first impression you have with one of their employees, because they will have on a uniform. That fact alone will cause you to think of them "differently," than another company in their respective fields.

In the course of doing business with them, you will notice how efficiently they operate. You will also save yourself time, by choosing to do business with them versus their competition. By adapting their services to your needs, you will feel as if their business was tailored especially for you.

And if in your business or your life, when you have an immediate need for their services, (any time day or night) your awful "ruin your day" experience would not turn out bad at all. You would be pleasantly surprised by the timeliness and the extra care that was taken on your behalf.

And if you didn't walk away feeling like an old friend just got you out of a jam, you did walk away with the feeling of being taken care of.

Notes:

CHAPTER SEVEN

A TEACHER, A BUSINESS OWNER AND A U.S. CONGRESSWOMAN

"The miracle power that elevates the few is found in their industry, application and perseverance, under the promptings of a brave determined spirit."

— **Mark Twain**
Author, (late 1800's early 1900's)

"Try not to become a person of success but rather a person of value."

— **Albert Einstein**
Nobel prize-winner physics (1921)

What do a teacher, a business owner and a U.S. Congresswoman have in common? They are all one in the same person. This individual is one of the most highly respected people in Fort Worth, as well as the entire state of Texas. She has also earned respect in Washington for her work fighting human trafficking, and her work on the Appropriations Subcommittees for Homeland Security, Labor-Health and Human Service-Education. Her story is a truly remarkable one as she went from being a single mother of three and teaching school to starting her own business.

I personally had the opportunity to see first hand the highest crime decrease in the nation during her term as mayor. Fort Worth also received the All America City Award during her tenure, which speaks to her influence on our city as well. While mayor, she founded the Business Assistance Center (BAC) and the Women's Business Center (WBC) which are centers located in Fort Worth that help establish and grow small businesses.

Coupled with her first-hand experience as a business owner and a politician known for getting the job done, I can't think of a better person to feature in my book.

ACHIEVEMENTS

Among her many achievements:
- Respected YMCA Congressional award for her support of anti-gang programs, 2004
- U.S. Chamber of Commerce Spirit of Enterprise Award Texas Women's Hall of Fame, 1999
- First woman to be named to the Fort Worth Business Hall of Fame, 1999
- James C. Howland Award for Urban Enrichment, 1994
- National Civic League All America City Award, 1993
- Rotary International Paul Harris Fellow Ward, 1993
- Distinguished Eastern Hills High School Graduate, 1992
- Texas Wesleyan University Outstanding Woman Graduate, 1991
- Texas Gridiron Club Female Newsmaker of the Year, 1990
- Zonata International Woman of the Year, 1990
- Business and Professional Woman of the Year, 1989

She was the first Republican woman to serve in the U.S. House of Representatives from Texas.

She is a member of the U.S. House of Representatives leadership, serving as a deputy majority whip. She is also the co-chair of the new and influential House and Senate Working Group on Aerospace and Defense, a special Congressional task force that recommends key policy decisions in the aerospace and defense sector to the full Congress. Additionally, she is House Speaker Dennis Hastert's appointee to the fifteen-member U.S. Air Force Academy Board of Visitors, an outside oversight board for the President of the United States and Congress.

She also serves on the powerful House Appropriations Committee and is an original member of the Select Committee on Homeland Security. She sits on two important Appropriations Subcommittees: Defense, and Labor-Health and Human Services-Education.

I am speaking of Congresswoman Kay Granger. A look back at her life makes one contemplate on how events often happen in life that become critical turning points that take us in a new and different direction.

In 1978, Kay was a newly divorced, single mother with a three-year old and six-month old twins. She was a high school teacher making $13,000 a year with the realization that her income would be inadequate to support her and her three children.

A psychologist friend of Kay's suggested she take a personality interest test to determine if she would be successful in business. The test was rather expensive, but Kay was in luck, as the junior college in Fort Worth, Tarrant County College (formerly Tarrant County Junior College), was offering the test for free. Kay remembers the test being very different than any other she had taken. Other career tests had shown that her skills were in the artistic fields. The results of this test however, showed an aptitude potential for self-employment and one of the industries recommended was as an insurance agent. The other recommended choices all required capital to start, which at the time, Kay did not have.

After researching various insurance companies, Kay selected a specific insurance company to work with. Kay shares what many of us who have chosen a career of self-employment want, to be compensated for how hard she worked.

THE GENDER BOX

The insurance and financial services industry has its own aptitude tests, the results of which are taken very seriously in the hiring process.

While filling out the questionnaire, Kay had one more stroke of luck: she inadvertently left both of the gender boxes blank. Remember, it was 1978, and given the corporate mindset toward women at the time, one has to wonder what the outcome would have been for Kay had she actually answered the gender question.

I feel fortunate that she and other women like her were determined to succeed and be role models for those in generations behind them. I feel lucky to have been born a decade or two later than her generation. I know I would have had to work harder to get where I am today if women like her hadn't paved the way.

When I attend meetings within the financial services industry and within our company, I usually scan the attendance list to get the percentage of women in attendance, and it varies from ten to twenty percent.

In Malcolm Gladwell's book *Blink,* he describes how we make subconscious decisions which are based on biases that at an early age are burned into our psyche. One of the most compelling stories in the book to illustrate this is when the author tests his own bias toward blacks versus whites by taking the test conducted at Harvard on this topic. Even more interesting is the fact that Malcolm is half white and half black. He took the test to try and convince himself that he didn't favor either race. But after taking the test numerous times, he succumbed to the fact that he has a bias, associating a higher percentage of positive words toward white over black people.

The research done in this area, toward our own bias, really made me wonder if Kay would have even been given a chance had she actually checked the gender box.

After Kay's test was sent and read by the insurance company's corporate offices, the word came back to Dallas, where Kay was based even though she resided in Fort Worth, to hire "him" immediately. The communication from corporate to Dallas was that they were very impressed with the results of the test, and even though the applicant left the gender boxes blank, it "could not possibly be a woman, so hire him immediately." The individual in charge of hiring let Kay know later that this correspondence had transpired.

Being in Fort Worth and all of the other agents in Dallas, it wasn't until several years later that Kay realized how few women were in the company. Because of her extreme success selling disability insurance, she was asked to speak at a five-state convention of insurance agents for the insurance company she was affiliated with. As she walked out on stage and looked out over the audience, 3,000 business suits and neckties stared back at her. It was not until that moment that she realized, she was the only woman agent in the room.

As she explained how there were very few other women in the insurance field at the time, I was trying to picture a single mom with three kids all under age three, starting a business. How on earth did she manage?

Kay decided to become a specialist in disability insurance and cater to the medical profession, primarily dentists. She would offer to speak to the graduating class of dentists on their need to insure their soon-to-be most valuable possession, their ability to earn a living. She realized that many of these doctors would be purchasing the practice of a retiring dentist, so she started working with retiring dentists and making sure their insurance needs were taken care of as well. Kay also worked with businesses like the Southland corporation doing life insurance planning.

SUCCESS AND HARD WORK

Kay developed strategic alliances with a CPA, an attorney, and a psychologist. I understood the retiring and the new dentist needing a CPA and an attorney, but I became very curious about why the psychologist? Kay explained that the psychologist was for the retiring business owners and executives to talk them through how they would handle retirement. I have felt for some time that some people don't know how to handle being retired.

So much of what we do and who we are as people comes from our profession. I have witnessed first hand people who have enough hobbies and interests that they comment on how they ever had enough time to work. While others, after a few months of retirement find themselves going back to work to "have something to do."

Kay said the psychologist would inquire about how the retiring business owner/executive thought he would spend retirement and the response would often be comments like "I think I'll play golf." After further inquiry and finding out that the business owner/executive didn't play much golf now, and if he did choose to play in retirement, two rounds a week still leaves a lot of free time. This made the business owner/executive realize the healthy thing to do was to explore other hobbies and interests. The retiring owner/executive would often stay several months to a few years before handing the practice over, which gave him time to explore their outside interests.

Kay's vision of the need for the psychologist is not only forward thinking, but also downright smart. I seriously doubt if her competitors had psychologists who met with their clients.

It is no wonder Kay became successful in selling insurance. If I were her client, that kind of special attention that had nothing to do with insurance and everything to do with what was important to me, would make me want to do business with her. I would also want to make sure the people in my world did business with her as well. I'm sure this kind of service and attention created advocates for Kay. These clients could tell that Kay cared about them, over and above her making a commission.

In addition to her three little ones, Kay's mother lived with Kay for eleven years, and though disabled, was able to help some at home with the children. Kay would study in the day when the kids were in day care, and see clients in the evening. Kay shared that when the children were a little older, she would tell them they were going on a field trip or vacation when Kay visited some of her clients.

They would trek across the state from Sugarland to Tyler to Austin. Kay would walk into her appointment and let the receptionist know that her children were going to wait in the reception area and color, while she talked to the doctor about his insurance. Of course at their young ages, the children didn't understand that their mom was actually working, but because Kay made a game of it, they found it fun.

I expect they now realize how hard their mom worked to provide for them, and imagine they have an enormous amount of respect for her.

The determination to succeed and the "accept no excuses" attitude that I have witnessed in other successful people, I saw in Kay too.

Kay clearly has a competitive spirit. She shared that during her career with this insurance company, about the only time she would loose on a business deal would be because the client wanted to go to one place to do all of their insurance business. So Kay went from being a captive agent with one insurance company, to starting her own independent insurance agency. And to comply with her client's requests, she added property and casualty lines of insurance.

POLITICAL CAREER

As Kay developed a reputation with many people in the community, she was able to serve on the city council. She chaired the zoning commission in 1981. At the time, Kay lived in east Fort Worth, one of the poorer areas with one of the highest crime rates. Her desire to serve in public office started from what she witnessed in east Fort Worth and what she thought could be done to "move that part of the city in a positive direction."

While serving on city council, Kay noticed that there was usually only one woman who served on each of the boards at the city. This group of women got together and discussed how they could promote more women to serve on boards. They decided that when a position came open, they would not only have a list of potential candidates that were qualified to fill the position, but they would also have resumes available. These women even offered to call these potential female candidates to see if they would consider the position. They became an advocate for these qualified women and the result is that more women started filling board positions.

Kay's reputation started to grow, and she was asked if she would be interested in being a part of Leadership Texas, to which she agreed. From there, when former Fort Worth mayor Bob Bolen announced that he would not run again, Kay decided to accept the challenge of running for mayor. Fort Worth has much to be thankful to her for, as our city has been blessed in part due to her leadership and vision.

Because of her success as mayor of Fort Worth, she came to know former congressman, Pete Geren. When Pete announced that he would not run again for congress, he told Kay that he would support her if she chose to run. Kay was up for the challenge.

THE GIRL FROM MOLDOVA

When I asked Kay, "What is the most rewarding thing you have ever done?" Kay replied, "Of course, it was very rewarding to see Fort Worth's crime drop by the largest percentage in the country while mayor and to see Fort Worth receive the All America City award during that time too."

Then she paused and smiled, her eyes sparkled, and I knew whatever was coming next was going to be something she was passionate about and very important to her. She told about how she had become involved in working to stop human trafficking, the sale of humans for sex and slave trade.

According to Kay, roughly 80 percent of those affected are women and children. Earlier in 2005, Kay had visited Moldova, which has a 40 percent unemployment rate and is the poorest area of Europe. Kay visited a hospital where the ramifications of the sex and slave trade could be witnessed first hand. While the doctor was giving her a tour, she saw a nineteen-year-old girl who was obviously bed-ridden. The doctor shared with Kay how this girl was kidnapped from Moldova and sent to Turkey with the promise of a job there. The "job" turned out to be living as a sex slave in a home in Turkey. She had tried to escape out of a six-story window and had fallen to the ground. As a result of the fall, her back was broken along with her pelvis and leg, and Kay was told she would never walk again.

When Kay asked what would happen to her, the doctor told her that pretty much what she saw would be "life" for this girl: a nineteen-year-old bedridden girl with no future.

Kay did not want to accept this as the final answer, so she got on the phone and called the Texas Back Institute in Dallas and spoke with a doctor there to see if through quality care, there might be hope for this little girl. The doctors at the Texas Back Institute confirmed that they felt there was.

Because of her extensive injuries, the cost to transport the girl was $80,000. With Kay's connections, the girl was transported at no cost to her or her family. The cost to treat her back, leg and pelvis was $350,000, all paid for by the Texas Back Institute. In October 2005, the girl from Moldova, who would "never walk again," walked herself onto a plane and headed back to her country.

Before she boarded her flight, Kay spoke with her. She told her that she was a very blessed little girl and she owed much to these doctors who treated her. Kay asked only two things of the girl: one, that she owed it to them to make something of her life; and two, that if the girl ever heard of anyone bad-mouthing the United States, she owed it to them to speak up and tell people how well she had been treated in the U.S.

For this little girl, meeting Kay was a turning point in her life. And I believe that through the connectivity of people, word-of-mouth advertising, advocate marketing or whatever you want to call it, she will do as Kay requested. And she will become an advocate for our United States.

Kay has a very tight schedule. My appointment with her was at 11:30 a.m., her 11 a.m. was promptly leaving as I arrived, and she had a noon appointment after our meeting. Our meeting ran over by fifteen minutes. Why? Because of Kay's obvious passion for the nineteen-year-old girl from Moldova and others like her. Kay's desire to stop human trafficking, and while doing so, create a positive image of the United States in our foreign allies minds.

BAC AND WBC

A word about the two centers Kay started while Mayor of Fort Worth: The Business Assistance Center (BAC) and The Women's Business Center (WBC). The success of these two centers has been so profound that they not only have been able to enlist the support of large corporations like Lockheed Martin and Chase Bank, but the federal government has used these centers as models for other cities to promote small business. (For more information on the BAC and WBC you can visit the website at www.fwbac.org)

Knowing that Kay is rarely able to physically be in her insurance office to oversee business because of her commitments in Washington, I knew that she had to have a great customer service policy in place. Part of my reason for interviewing her was to find out how she managed the business, when she was rarely able to be present.

Attributes That Create Advocate Marketing

Q: What do you feel is your differentiating factor that sets you apart from your competition?

A: The personal attention that we give all of our insurance clients. We are very accessible to them and we really get to know them, their needs and what they want so that we can truly take care of them.

Q: Do you feel you have developed customer loyalty?

A: The response to the last question could be the same for this one. We really know our clients and their needs so well that we anticipate their needs before they ask. Because of this, they walk away feeling like they have been taken care of.

Q: What do you do to save the customer time?

A: Our company keeps meticulous and detailed records on every client. We don't want our clients to waste their valuable time repeating information that is already on file. Because of our detailed record keeping, our staff calls the client several months before their actual annual review date, so they don't have to remember when the date is.

If you are a client of our company, we think in advance for you, so you don't have to, which certainly provides our clients with peace of mind. (This reminds me of the part of the Ritz-Carlton creed that states to anticipate the clients needs, before they ask). Our policy is to offer and visit the client's office whenever possible, to allow them to maximize their time on their business.

Q: Describe what you feel is the customer "experience."

A: We have trained all of our staff to if at all possible, contemplate putting themselves in their customer's shoes. I also have trained them to understand the needs of the small business owner so that they can relate to the client as much as possible. (This is also a quality that the Ritz-Carlton deems important when delivering their royal experience).

Q: Has your product or service been customized or personalized for your customer?

A: When I was actively presenting to clients I made it a point to read the client during the interview. I was always prepared to give all of the details if that is what the client wanted, but if the client wanted the bottom line only, I would present only the basics. This would customize each presentation to each client based on that client's personality. I have trained my staff to do the same.

I would show them what needed to be implemented immediately and then as their company grew the logical services that would be put in place for them depending on their needs and the type of business they were in.

Q: Do your employees feel "a part of the company" so much that they will treat your customer the same whether you are present or not?

A: Being gone for so much of the time, this was a very important thing for me to establish. To help them feel involved, when I am home I communicate with the staff at my company, what I am working on in Congress. This helps my staff feel apart of the important committees that I serve on.

(With this kind of involvement, I can see how her staff would want to help her company continue its success, knowing that Kay is working hard to improve the state of our country and improve our U. S. image abroad.)

Q: Can you recall a time when you made a mistake with your customer and they overlooked it and continued to do business with you despite the mistake?

A: I have instilled in all of my staff to take ownership of whatever mistake is made immediately to have the best chance of appeasing our customers.

Q: Do you have any other comments about customer service that you would like to share?

A: In my business and in politics I teach my staff to search for the "personal" reason that is the basis for the complaint. Our political office receives on average 250 letters a week. Our staff responds to every one of them. (This is somewhat amazing when you consider that, after the anthrax scare, all of her mail is sent to Washington to be inspected before being sent to her office in Fort Worth.)

Myself and my staff look for the personal reason that is the basis for the issue that is being brought to our attention. Once it is found, we empathize first with the personal tragedy that often prompts the letter and then state why the issue can or cannot be addressed.

In addition to Kay being the mother of three children, her eldest son J.D. and twins Brandon and Chelsea, she is also a grandmother of two, Jack and Logan. In 2006, we are all in for a treat, as she will add "author" to her many titles and accomplishments. Her book on patriotism is due out July 4, 2006.

It is hard not to like someone who works hard, is determined, and has a passion for something they believe in. I admired Kay for those attributes and her success in business before the interview, and my admiration grew stronger after speaking with her.

And in the future, if there is a ballot box with Kay's name next to it, I'll make certain that it doesn't go unmarked.

Notes:

CONCLUSION

"The only thing that separates winners from losers is, winners take action!

— **Anthony Robbins**
Motivational speaker and author (1990's/2000's)

"The greatest pleasure in life is doing what people say you cannot do."

— **Walter Bagehot**
Respected journalist (1800's)

"Just do it."

— **Nike**
Advertising campaign

Hopefully as a consumer, this book has inspired you to do business with the companies that, by their actions and how they treat you, communicate that they are worthy of your business.

As an employee, you will want to work for companies that treat you the way you deserve to be treated.

As a business owner or manager, I hope you have been inspired and have learned from the companies referenced in these pages, on what to do and what not to do to create customer advocates.

Whether you own a dry cleaners, automotive repair, or sandwich shop, I hope you will develop your own customer service policy and your own advocate marketing plan. Hopefully you will want to implement things to "wow" your customer, and I'm confident that you will reap the rewards on your bottom line for doing so.

I also hope you will develop rewards for your employees, so they will feel "a part of" your company and a part of the positive "experience" that you are creating for your customer. I have no doubts that by making your employees feel appreciated, you will inspire them to care about the experience you want for your customers. Your customers will in turn want their family and friends to "experience" your company as well. As a result, you will not only have more fun in your business but will also be rewarded by an increase in profits.

We are surely in agreement that implementing small and quite possibly inexpensive things that save the customer time, make them feel special and become your differentiating feature, will be what produces large benefits for your business.

Through the connectivity of the advocates we create, our "stories" will contagiously spread with an ounce of "ring around the rosy" ramifications. It is becoming increasingly evident, that now more than ever, word-of-mouth advertising is not only the least expensive but also the only advertising, that really works. If you don't want to take my word for it, take the word of those advocate-marketing imposters who are paid to pose as advocates for large corporations.

Ok, now I am going to ask you for a favor. I don't have a million dollar marketing budget for this book. Through the connectivity of the people you know, I know you know others who would benefit from reading this book. So the favor is to ask you to buy a copy of this book for the favored people in your world. Buying books for others will help further prove my theory that advocate marketing really works and at the same time allow others to benefit from what you have just experienced.

Over the next twenty years, you and I have a huge opportunity to grow our businesses with passionate customer service and our advocate marketing plans. As respected author and economist Harry

Dent said about the impact of the baby boomer generation on our future, they as a group of consumers are "like a pig moving through a python." "They will drive the greatest economic boom in our history."

We will continue to change and consume what is important and what becomes important to us. We will need great companies to change with us and provide us with what we want and need, delivering it to us in a like manner. And as for me, a baby boomer and consumer myself, I hope I will hear more and more often, "Wow, what was the name of that company?"

Rebecca D. Turner, ChFC

- Recognized as one of the Great Women of Texas, November 2003.
- Business Assistance Center (BAC) Board member since 1999.
- Leadership Fort Worth Class of 1999.
- United Way of Metropolitan Tarrant County-Exemplary Community Stewardship through Leadership Giving.
- National Association of Women in Construction, Past President and member since 1995.
- Publicized in Builder Architect magazine and The Image, (a NAWIC publication).
- American Cancer Society (Sword of Hope Award), 1995.

www.rebeccaturner.com

ABOUT THE AUTHOR

"Some people enter our lives and leave almost instantly. Others stay, and forge such an impression on our heart and soul, we are changed forever."

— **Author Unknown**

"There are essentially two things that will make you wiser, the books you read and the people you meet."

— **Charles Tremendous Jones**
Known as one of the most dynamic speakers
in our country over the last fifty years

Just so you know, what you are about to read has nothing to do with customer service.

EVERYONE HAS A STORY

I am not writing this because my story is so important, but because everyone has a story and this is mine. I feel compelled to share my story with you for three reasons. One is that my life is not so exciting that one day someone will want to write my biography. So I figure over the next few pages is my only chance to tell my story. Secondly, I consulted many clients, friends and local authors on this journey I've had of writing. And many of them encouraged me to write about my life. So here it is, and for those of you who encouraged me, I have one thing to say, "Be careful what you ask for."

Third and most importantly, I hope that this will motivate you to write your own story. Homer Hickman, author of memoirs and other fine books, states "There are stories inside each of us that wait like magic spirits to be released from our hearts." And Frank P. Thomas, who wrote *How To Write Your Life Story*, and who has read thousands of manuscript pages of people's lives, states that he has "seen an instinctive urge deep in the heart of people to learn more about who they are and where they come from." He calls personal memoirs "a precious document that can live in your family for generations."

I'm sure there is someone in your life that will appreciate your taking the time to write about your life. And certainly no one can tell your story like you can.

BEING ADOPTED

I was born in Topeka, Kansas in 1963. My biological mother was twenty-two and unmarried when she had me. I would later learn why she gave me up for adoption. She didn't know my father, and she felt in her words that I had a "better chance at life" if I could grow up with both a mom and a dad. She also said she didn't think it was right or fair of her to keep me.

Coincidentally, at age twenty-two, I decided to contact her, for one main reason, to tell her "thank you" for having me. I imagined through her life she had wondered to herself if she had done the right thing by putting me up for adoption. I wanted to assure her she had. I had a wonderful life with my mom, dad and brother and sister.

I contacted the Kansas Children's Service League to find out how to contact my mom. Their policy was that they would look in my file to see if there was a forwarding address for her. If there was, then that meant she wanted to be contacted, if there was no address, then she didn't. Fortunately, there was an address.

You often hear stories of people searching for years and spending all kinds of money trying to find their parents. Well, I guess I was lucky. Within a week, I received a letter back from her. And when I got to the bottom of the letter I had to smile; she signed her name, "Dorothy." But what other name would she have had, to be the mother of a little girl who grew up in Kansas and was living for the most part, a fairy tale life?

She told me in her letter how she thought of me every year on my birthday, which surprised me. I wasn't around to remind her of the day and to celebrate it. So I never once considered that she would remember my birthday. I think that made me feel special.

She sent me a photo and described herself as 4'11" with black hair and sharp blue eyes. Her heritage was French, American Indian, and Irish. Of course, that is only half of my biological story, and I have to admit that I was a little disappointed when she told me that she didn't know much about my father. She only said that he was athletic, muscular, good looking, and apparently, irresistible.

EVERYTHING HAPPENS FOR A REASON

We never did meet, and unfortunately I have lost her information. But I do believe everything happens for a reason. She told me after reading my letter that she knew her prayers had been answered and that she had made the right decision by giving me up for adoption. It made me feel good that I could help her be at peace with this decision she had made in her life.

"YOU'RE ADOPTED?"

My mom and dad kept a storybook that described how they "picked" me out and took me home. At the end of the book was a photo of me. They were so matter of fact about it, that I never wondered much about "adoption" until attending school and kids would say "You're adopted?" with surprise in their voice. Their questions about it always surprised me. The way my parents explained how they adopted me seemed so normal, and I accepted it as such. They told me how they went to an agency, kind of like a store, and picked me out.

My sister had been adopted two years before me, so for a long time adoption was the only way I knew how you had children. It wasn't until kids questioned me about adoption that I started to wonder about it. If you aren't "picked" out, how else do you show up in life? So even though they explained to me what adoption was, I didn't know how it was different than how everyone else arrived here in the world.

In the early '60s, adoption was not as common as today, and some parents who adopt would choose not to tell their children about the adoption. It was a little taboo and somehow I think society felt sorry for parents who "had" to adopt, because they couldn't have their own children. To make it "easier" on the parents, agencies would often try to match eye and hair color of the adopting parents to the baby. In fact, both of my parents had blue eyes and dark hair, as I do.

MY PERCEPTION OF THE WORLD

I guess for most of my life, and maybe this was the start of my perception of the world, I've felt the glass is half full, not half empty. I figured being adopted was a good thing. I mean, someone didn't want me and then someone did. So that's a wash, right? How is that bad? To this day, there is a special place in my heart for people who adopt. Besides, if my parents had to pick me out of a baby line up, I must have been the cutest and best looking baby for them to pick me over all of the others. I think this gave me a healthy ego, and it also was one more thing in my life that made me feel special.

MY MOM'S INFLUENCE

Growing up, my mom made it very clear that there was a wrong way and then my mom's way of doing things.

She was meticulous about our home being clean, very organized and always presentable in case someone would drop by unannounced.

My mom was also adamant that we were properly dressed for whatever the occasion and she taught us to take pride in our appearance.

In my mom's world, everything had its place in the house and I could retire now if I had a dollar for every time she told us "put things back where they belong."

Being a little opinionated and a little stubborn are traits my mom and I have in common. And since we didn't always share the same opinion, a conflict between us would often arise as a result. Because she felt so strongly about many of her beliefs, she would challenge me on my views when we didn't agree. I realize now that this actually helped me form my own opinions and beliefs by defending them. It made me realize what I did believe in, and I am very thankful for her influence.

I have more discipline, more determination and a strong sense of what I believe in because of her. I'm not the most organized person you'll ever meet, but I'm less disorganized because of her influence on my life.

Because of my mom, birthdays were highly celebrated and the person with the birthday was made to feel special. We were able to choose themes for our birthdays, which often would include an elaborate and detailed cake to match the theme.

Breakfast, lunch and dinner at our house were always with us seated around the dinner table. It is interesting the effect I now know that had on my life. At a square or round table you sit directly across from someone, which makes it easy to look them in the eye and talk about the day's events or whatever was on your mind. From others' accounts of growing up, I'm not so sure that this practice was or is the norm. But I think it was good for us, as it helped our family talk more and it gave me a feeling of security and stability.

My mom was very strict about the amount of television we were allowed to watch. She called it the "boob tube." We were allowed thirty minutes each day. And on the weekend or special occasions we might be allowed longer. When she would leave the house for an errand she would take a tube from the back of the television to insure we wouldn't watch it while she was gone.

I certainly don't win at television trivia games but I'm thankful for her limiting our viewing time. My brother and I spent more time outside playing and interacting, which was good for us. My sister chose to spend her time reading and as a result, she is an avid reader with a large vocabulary.

FOND MEMORIES AND PHOTO ALBUMS

Our home wasn't the only thing that my mom was detailed and organized about. My brother, sister and I all have several complete photo albums and scrap books. These albums detail the place and date of birthdays, band trips, vacations or other life events that she wanted us to have a memory of.

My parents believed in the family vacation. Every summer we would pack the station wagon full of food for the road and beam in anticipation of what we were going to do and see on our trip.

Without CDs, cassettes, eight tracks or MP3 players, the radio was about all there was to listen to and I remember that it didn't work very well, anyway, so it was usually turned off. To pass the time, we would sing songs, often hymns that we knew from church, or play road games that my parents made up.

Most of us probably have a "story" that our parent repeatedly told about us that was their favorite. For my dad, mine must have been when we were on a family vacation, I was a few years old and we were at the hotel pool. I was sitting on the edge of the water, my dad was close by but I managed to jump in and proceeded to sink right to the bottom of the pool. My dad quickly went down after me, pulled me up and sat me back on the side of the pool. Since I had swallowed water, I was coughing and spitting it up in attempts to breathe. As he was getting out, still spitting up water I promptly jumped right back in. Needless to say, my dad felt it best that we go back to the room. My parents recognized my fearless and unpredictable nature and realized they would have to keep a close eye on me.

My parents knew they were building memories for us and I believe that was their intent. I know they sacrificed by doing the things that would be fun for us, but not necessarily fun for them.

My father loved Colorado so that is where we went most summers. When I was twelve we started going in the winter too so we could snow ski. We would stay in condos that had kitchens. I remember my mom making casseroles for breakfast and dinner. She would freeze them, pack them in the cooler and even put the date the dish was to be served on top of each container.

My father was very involved in the Kansas Savings and Loan Association. As a result he would often travel. Wherever he went, even on short trips, he would always bring something back for us. I would get excited about something as simple as the pens with liquid and a floating object inside of them. I thought "how exciting to go and visit different cities."

My dad would also bring me a bar of soap from the hotel where he had stayed. At the time, the hotels would have a drawing or picture imprinted on the paper that wrapped the soap. I don't know why I kept them but I had a large shoebox full of soaps that I kept into my adulthood. Maybe they were little reminders of these exciting places he had been and a reminder that he thought of me and made me feel special.

As a child I thought, "If I can't do what he did for a living so I can go to exciting places then I'll be a truck driver." In my little mind, I thought that would be a good way to "see the world."

I also remember in second or third grade when the teacher asked us to each state what we wanted to be when we grew up. I remember saying a "millionaire." Everyone laughed, but I was serious. Obviously at the time my ambition for wealth (so I could do whatever I wanted whenever I wanted), and my career choice didn't necessarily match.

ABOUT THE AUTHOR

THE MIDDLE OF NOWHERE

Most of my life growing up was spent in a small town in the middle of nowhere in Kansas; Lyons, Kansas to be exact. I call it the middle of nowhere because if you wanted to go to the mall or a movie, you were in the car for an hour to get there.

To further illustrate the meaning of the phrase "the middle of nowhere," in a travel book I highly recommend, *Road Trip USA,* the author describes a highway that goes right through the middle of the state and thus through the middle of Lyons. It is US 56, and the author labels it "the loneliest road in America." I think you get my point. There are however two stop lights as you pass through on highway 56, so you won't necessarily "miss it," but it is a small dot on the map.

"THERE'S NO PLACE LIKE HOME"

There is openness to the sky and countryside in Kansas that I actually miss. In fact, it is funny how I thought I would never miss the openness of the country, but I do. And now that I live in Fort Worth, if I drive an hour in the right direction, I can see openness that reminds me of home. It is interesting that growing up we would drive an hour to "be" somewhere, and now I enjoy driving an hour to see nothing but countryside and sky.

Now that I think back to when I was young, we would spend many a night sitting on the back of my dad's car looking up at the sky, especially on stormy nights. The openness in Kansas causes you to instinctively look up as you walk outside. I heard once that more native Kansans are in the aeronautical field than from any other state.

Not that Fort Worth is a huge city, but the sky does get lost with the lights of downtown and the buildings that are there.

My dad was a banker, and I suppose we were considered upper middle class in the tight knit community of Lyons. We were members

138

of the nine-hole grass green country club (I say grass green because in the smaller towns there were actually sand greens and you had to rake the sand on the green, after you finished putting on them). So we all thought we had something special, with our country club with grass greens. Many people were members of the country club just for the social membership, so they would have a nice place to eat on Saturday night without needing to leave town.

RANDOM THOUGHTS

For some of us, those sixty-thousand random thoughts that scientists tell us that we have each day are more often and more random. Looking back on my elementary school days, I never really excelled in school. I think my teachers would continue to pass me because I did show up for class. However, paying attention when I got there was another story. My parents even took me to a specialist to find out why I didn't do well in school. He was at a loss after my examination. I'm sure I had and still have attention deficit disorder. I'm also relatively sure, from the stories, I am the hyperactive type.

Of course they didn't know what to do with that disorder at the time, nor did they even know what it was. So I learned to adapt, but school was always hard for me. Even though I know now, of course, that I am intelligent, at the time the way teaching and testing was done, and with my attention problem, the results appeared as though I wasn't intelligent.

It took me years to get over my insecurity and to realize I was actually smart; it just didn't seem that way at the time. Also, as a child when an adult tells you something, you accept what they say as the truth without challenging them. So I bought in to what I was told by adults, that I just probably wasn't going to be able to do much, because I was a "little slow." I was told to not expect to go to college and to try and find something I enjoyed, that wasn't going to require much schooling past high school.

EDUCATION

I did finish my bachelor's degree at Kansas State University in '85, and in '94 I earned a degree as a chartered financial consultant from The American College, in Bryn Mawr, Pennsylvania. That degree was very important to me. Because I always questioned myself and my intelligence, it was important to me to earn a degree in what I do every day—financial advising. In fact, as a reward when I finished, I went out and bought myself a new car.

In elementary school, since I didn't picture myself good in school work, I made it my goal every day to see if I could crack the teacher up and get them to laugh. If I did that I thought, then it was a successful day. Many of the days I was able to accomplish my goal of making the teacher laugh and I was labeled the class clown. Since I was a little disruptive, consequently most of my elementary school years my desk was right next to the teacher.

When I made it to junior high, my studies caught up with me, and I wasn't prepared for the junior high math class. So I was put in a slow math class. Believe it or not, there were actually teachers that made fun of us in the class as well as other students. To make matters worse the "slow" class was way at the end of the hall, and you had to pass all the other classrooms as you went to it. I remember feeling like everyone was watching the dummies go down the hall while all the "normal" kids entered the "normal" classrooms. There was a teacher at the end of the hall in the classroom right next to ours who taught the normal math class. He would stand outside of his doorway with his hands on his hips. As we walked past him, it was very intimidating, and I remember feeling like he was looking at us like we were big losers. He would even make reference to us in his class; when someone didn't get a certain topic, that if they weren't careful, he would "make them go next door with the dummies."

"RIGHT" SIDE OF THE TRACKS

As a result of being in the class, my self esteem suffered, but I am grateful that I had the experience. In a town of 3,000 there was an unspoken hierarchy from which side of the tracks you lived on, and what your dad did for a living. Everyone knew both of those things about you when they met you. So my dad being a banker and living right next to the country club, everyone knew we were on the "right" side of the tracks. What was interesting was there was no one in the slow math class but me, who was considered to live on the "right" side of the tracks.

This experience made me realize how much people in general are alike. We all have some of the same wants and desires. And if you remember your junior high days, fitting in and being accepted were pretty high up on the list. I think this experience humbled me, and made me realize I was no better or worse than anyone else. Some of the kids in this class became my good friends. I probably would not have taken the opportunity to socialize with them, had it not been for this experience.

I realized how others treated them differently because of their situation. This experience created a desire in me to want to treat others fairly and as equals no matter what their circumstances.

I'm sure if you grew up in a small town this brings back memories. In school we were all classified as a part of a group. And I think society in general is comfortable putting us in a group and are not comfortable if they don't know where we fit in. When I went on to high school, I kept in contact with some of the kids from our slow math class. We had bonded. I remember sitting with them before school started. As you walked into school, everyone sits in their respective groups. When I would sit with them, my other friends would be curious as to why.

I hated conformity anyway, and hated that others thought they were better just because of where they were in life. I remember being up for homecoming queen, and thinking how surprised some of the kids were about that. I certainly didn't fit the typical "beauty queen." They were even more surprised when I, probably because I had the broadest cross section of friends, won by a popular vote.

Sports came natural to me as I was pretty athletic. Sports are where I excelled, and at the time probably saved me from being a slacker at everything else in my life. At the time, being successful at something helped my self-esteem.

I remember one time in kindergarten, I decided a certain boy in my class was "the" boy that I wanted to "go with." I remember announcing this to my mom when I got home from school one day. The boy's last name concerned my mom as he had many older brothers whose names were often in the paper for various petty crimes and for spending the night in jail. I remember her inquiry as to what on earth made me think that this was the boy to "go with." I informed her that I had challenged all the boys in class to a foot race, and he was the only one who could beat me. I thought that made him pretty cool.

Knowing my mom, she probably rolled her eyes and said, "Oh, brother." I'm sure she wondered what on earth was in store for her with a little girl who picked her boyfriends by the manner I just described.

Looking back on how my life has transpired, I know that I prefer challenges to not being challenged, and I get bored or just don't have fun unless something is challenging to me.

HE BELIEVED IN ME

My father was wise and taught me how to play golf at age five. I started competing in the junior golf program not long after that. I had early success at golf. As you can imagine in the late '60s and early '70s, I didn't have much competition as a girl playing golf in the middle of Kansas. I can't ever remember losing at these junior golf tournaments, and even when they put me with the boys, I often won. I guess in my little mind I developed this idea that I was really good, since almost no one my age anyway, could beat me.

One of my fondest memories of playing with my dad was when

we were at a savings and loan meeting at the Broadmoor in Colorado Springs one summer. Dad had a meeting in the morning and then we had a tee time that afternoon. They paired us with two men my dad did not know from another state.

If you are a golfer, you know that the men's tees are furthest from the hole and so men tee off first, and the ladies tees are forward so women tee off last. As my dad stood on the men's tee box with these two men, they didn't even try to hide how disgusted they were to be paired with a ten-year-old on the golf course, and a girl at that! My dad teed off last and without looking at them as he teed up his ball he said, "Don't worry if she slows us up, I'll make her pick up her ball."

As we drove to my tee box after everyone else had hit, I remember being very nervous feeling pressure to hit a good drive. My dad must have sensed this as he reassured me stating, that "I had nothing to worry about." I did hit a good drive, and it was in the fairway, which neither of the men had done. It was also further than the two men and further than the difference in distance between the men's and women's tees.

As I got in on my side of the golf cart, my father laughed and stated "I don't think we will hear anything from them today." I remember how good it felt that he believed in me, when at the time, I didn't have the confidence to believe in myself.

Since I had some success at sports, I would practice often in my two favorite sports, basketball and golf. I would spend hours shooting baskets in our driveway. My dad even put a light out by the goal, so I could practice when it was dark. This didn't please my mom, as she wanted me to be a "well rounded" person, and thought that I spent enough time shooting during daylight hours.

On Saturday mornings when the sun was up, I would play eighteen holes of golf, often with my little brother, and be back home by the time the morning cartoons were on. Often my dad would come home from work in the evening, and we would grab a couple clubs to carry with us and walk across the creek from our house to play a few holes.

We would play as many holes as we could, until it was so dark we couldn't see the ball anymore.

Even today, when the sun is setting, and it is considered dusk, I often think of my dad. Especially if I can smell fresh cut grass or hear locust chirping, I think of the times I spent with him. It is funny how a smell or sound can take you back to a certain time in your life.

Even though it is sad to be without him, I'm thankful for the memories and these things that "take me back," so I will never forget.

In Dr. Sylvia Rimm's book *See Jane Win,* her study was done on 1,000 girls who grew up in the '60s and became successful. Many of the girls had similar experiences, but there was one event that they all had independently experienced. It was that someone in their life, when they were slacking off, let them know that they knew they were better than they were acting. In a way, these adults were letting the children know that they believed in them, more than the child was at that time in their life, believing in themselves. I believe this happened to me as well with my father and a few of my teachers and coaches at different times in my life.

THE POWER OF INTENTION

I think that sports can really prepare you for life and for a career. It requires teamwork, goal setting and discipline, all of which are needed to succeed in business. I feel that those attributes help me now in my business. It would be hard to be self-employed without discipline. It would also be hard to run our practice without good teamwork. I am adamant about setting goals for myself, and grew up learning to do that through sports. I remember going to a basketball camp and learning about the power of the mind through psycho cybernetics. The concept of this was a revelation to me. I used this in sports, envisioning the basketball going through the net or the golf ball landing in the cup and hearing the sound that it makes.

To this day, I visualize events before they happen. I practice the positive outcome in my mind to enhance my chances of success in a particular matter. A book I recently read is kind of a psycho cybernetics revisited, *The Power of Intention*, by Dr. Wayne Dyer. Dr. Dyer has read hundreds of books on the psychology, sociology, and spiritual aspects of intention by both modern and ancient scholars.

His research reveals "a fairly common definition of intention as a strong purpose or aim, accompanied by a determination to produce a desired result." Dyer goes on to say "if you are one of those people with a never-give-up attitude combined with an internal picture that propels you toward fulfilling your dreams, you fit this description of someone with intention."

Furthermore, Dyer illustrates these people are "super-achievers and probably proud of their ability to recognize and take advantage of opportunities that arise." Dyer describes people who live at high levels of intention as people who have made themselves available for success. He calls these people "connectors."

To connectors, it all seems so simple: "keep your thoughts on what you intend to create." "They perceive seemingly insignificant events as being orchestrated in perfect harmony. To connectors, everything that shows up in their life is there because the power of intention intended it to be."

By thinking positively and focusing on what I intend to have happen in my life, I have been able to accomplish almost everything that I have set out to do.

COLLEGE SCHOLARSHIP

After winning the Kansas state golf tournament my sophomore, junior and senior years, golf "seemed" too easy. So when I graduated from high school, instead of playing golf in college, I accepted a scholarship to play basketball at a junior college. Talk about a challenge, a 5'3 inch tall white point guard?

During my collegiate basketball career, I rarely encountered anyone as short as I was. I loved doing the unexpected, and I averaged 3-5 rebounds a game during my career. Basketball did pay for the first two years of my education, and I was thankful for that. I didn't want my parents to be burdened with the expense, and I didn't want to accumulate debt either.

WE'RE NOT IN KANSAS ANYMORE

After finishing junior college I earned a bachelor degree at Kansas State University. I knew that I wanted to move to an exciting city that would hopefully have more opportunities for a career for me than in a small town in Kansas. I knew two people I could live with in two of the cities that I thought would be exciting and opportunistic, Dallas and Denver. I sent over 100 letters with resumes and followed up with them all by phone. I struck out as not one of the companies was interested in hiring me. This was a very frustrating experience, as I always felt I would be good at something, I just didn't know what.

CHALLENGING MYSELF PHYSICALLY

I ended up with my first job managing a health club that was a national chain at the time. I did this for two years while I fulfilled one of my dreams, which was to try bodybuilding and power lifting. It was the mid '80s and in this area, there were many trainers to pick from and places to get advice and help in competing. I competed only one time in power lifting, and really only because I was working out one day and a power lifting trainer noticed how much I was bench pressing.

He approached me and asked, "Have you ever thought of competing?" I said that I had always wanted to, but didn't know how to train for it. He said he would love to train me at no charge and if I would give him three months he would increase my bench to 250 pounds. So after doing whatever he told me to do, I competed one time in Tyler, Texas. I remembered benching 242.5 lbs. Afterwards everyone wanted to know "who I was." I explained that it was the first time I had competed and probably the last, as I had been dared to do it and to see how much I could do.

I found out later that the state record for my weight class, 148 lbs., was 220 pounds. And the weight I lifted for the bench would have put me second in the nation. My record didn't count because I didn't do the dead lift or squat. I found out later that I could have just done the bar so it would have counted (but I didn't know that at the time.) The experience did give me personal satisfaction because I know what I did and it was fun to accept the challenge.

I competed three times in bodybuilding and qualified to attend national competitions. I really had done what I wanted, which was to see how far I could push myself athletically. I also was able to test my will and determination. It is a very grueling and hard sport. Because of the dieting, it isn't just a sport, but a new way of life. I'm thankful for the experience and what it taught me, but I realized at my last competition that I had gone as far as I could go naturally. I wasn't interested in taking drugs to enhance my chances and could tell that the other competitors had. The drugs were easy to get at the time as well.

With the realization of not competing anymore, I knew I needed to get a "real" job and start a career. On a side note, I'd like to share something that for some reason people find interesting about me. When you play the game, "tell the group something that they don't know about you and would be surprised about," besides my being a "homecoming queen," remember the cheesy reality game, that no one wants to admit they ever watched, *American Gladiator?*" Well, I was a contestant, and people seem amused by that.

MY FIRST "REAL" JOB

Back to my career, I received a job doing the payroll for a trucking company, and it was at night from 5:30 p.m. to 3 a.m. I did this for about two years, as I was still searching for what I really wanted to do. A friend at the time was an assistant to Willie Cox, a financial advisor, and I was offered a part time day job as an assistant there, for a man named Ken Comer. I worked from 9 a.m. until 3 p.m. for him and then went to the trucking company to do payroll. This went on for a year. The first week on the job as an assistant, Ken told me he was going on vacation, and he handed me the phone book and said, "See if you can set some appointments for me, for when I get back."

To his amazement, I had several meetings lined up for him when he returned. I think he just gave me the phone book thinking, it wouldn't hurt, but really didn't think I'd set any appointments. He asked me what on earth I had told them, that they wanted to meet with him. I told him that when I called people, I let them know that you were honest and trustworthy, and it would be worth fifteen minutes of their time to see if you could help them, like you have helped other business owners just like them.

I guess this impressed him and he started bugging me about becoming a financial advisor myself.

A PERFECT SCORE

At the time, there was a personality test that was given to potential advisors. The test was supposed to determine, based on your personality, if you would be good as an advisor. The industry believed in the test so strongly that even if you were considered unlikely to succeed, if you did well on the test, you were often hired. After much prodding by Ken, I gave in and took the test. I prayed about God opening or closing a door for me with the results of the test being a sign. Well, it was a fluke. I am sure, as I received a perfect score. So, unwillingly, I might add, I kept my commitment that if I did well, I would "try" it.

So starting with a phone book, a cubicle and an extreme fear of failing, I was determined to make it in this business.

ACHIEVEMENT JUNKIE

Looking back on my life, I realize now that I was an achievement junkie. I just didn't feel good about myself unless I was achieving something. It didn't matter what success I had in the past. I felt like a mouse in a cage on a metal wheel and I couldn't afford to step out of the wheel and stop spinning. I had to achieve something in the here and now to feel good about myself.

It wasn't until this point in my life that I realized the difference in self-confidence and self esteem. I had one, self-confidence, because of my achievements, but not the other, self esteem. Fifteen years ago I read a book that changed my life, *The Search for Significance,* by Robert S. McGee. He describes all of the traps we put ourselves in to feel we have self-worth. I was in the achievement trap.

The book goes on to say that the reason we are all equal and have self-worth is because we all have the same opportunity to accept that Christ died for our sins and accepting that fact alone is the reason for our salvation. There is nothing we can do to one up one another or to improve on the grace through Christ's death, that has been given to all of us.

THE MOST REWARDING THINGS I HAVE EVER DONE

So knowing that for most of my life I have been an achievement junkie, you might find it interesting that the most rewarding things I have done were not achievements at all. And just as when I interviewed Kay Granger and asked her the most rewarding thing she had ever done, for me, too, it had to do with the people and relationships in my life. When you write "your story" you will most likely find this to be true for you as well.

One of the most rewarding events in my life was the years I had the privilege of helping raise a teenager, Erica Salazar, and help her mature into a young woman.

The other event was when I had the fortunate opportunity to take care of my mother in the last several months of her life as she battled breast cancer. When this experience was over, I felt as if I had lived my whole life for this one task of helping my mom be as comfortable as possible, enjoy her last few months of life on this earth and help her prepare to go from this life to the next.

Witnessing the way she kept her positive attitude, maintained her sense of humor and was so unselfish was a privilege in itself. She made me realize how futile it is to complain about a situation as she graciously accepted where she was and made the best of it. She made me want to make the best of any situation that I might encounter in the future. And if I ever have to cross the horrible bridge of terminal cancer, that if I could have half her courage, half as much of her unselfishness, and half as much of her sense of humor, then I truly will have accomplished something.

If you ever have the opportunity to help someone you care about go through the dying process, do it. I was very apprehensive and it isn't fun by any means, but I'm certain it will be rewarding and you will be glad you did it. (A book that helped me through this process is *Mid Wife For Souls*, by Kathy Kalina.)

Everyone has people in their lives who have made them better than they would have been without them. These are those people in my life and this book is dedicated to them.

My God and Savior Jesus Christ.

My dad who believed in me before I believed in myself, and my mother who taught me discipline and to care about my reputation and my appearance. You both taught me to work hard and to practice in what I wanted to excel, and that if I did, it would pay off.

Thanks to my brother Barton because you are eight years younger than me and were a little parrot, repeating everything I said. I was a better person, knowing you looked up to me. To my sister Beth thanks for being my sister and sharing your kids with me. Rose Turner, thanks for putting up with my brother. You are truly one of the best things that has ever happened to him, and I appreciate you and am glad you are part of our family.

Thank you to my niece and nephews, Amber, David, Kelsey, Jordan and my friends Erica Salazar and her daughter Emilie. You all made me want to be a better person so I could be a good example to you.

To my friend Monica Ray, thanks for your friendship. My grandparents who taught me how to work hard, have fun, love God, and helped inspire me to want to be self-employed and I thank them for it.

Mary Lou Frazier, and the whole Frazier clan, thanks for making me a part of your family and for sharing your love of golf with me.

To my good friend Lewis Runnion, thanks for being supportive and finding Ken Stone for me. Ken, thanks for the use of your arm!

Thanks to my friends Nancy Duncan and Terri King for their friendship and letting me stay at their cabin. I started and finished my book at your cabin and what better place for inspiration to write.

To two of my dearest and long time Fort Worth friends Theresa Loving and Karine Moe, thanks for your friendship, for always being able to pick up where we left off and never letting anything get in the way of us being friends.

Carol Glover, thanks for all of your time and interest in my dream. Rhonda Lombardo, you don't know it, but you were the first friend who I felt loved and accepted me, just the way I am. Jamie and Jeff Webb, thanks for putting up with me for seventeen years and for being good friends. Julie (Crane) Mall, Ben Vasconcells and Bruce Snyder, thanks for helping me make it through grade school and junior high.

Fernandez Cafe (Vickery Blvd., Fort Worth, Texas) thanks for serving such great food and providing a home away from home for me.

My business partners, James Taylor, Allison Norman and Brandon Howard, thanks to all of you for understanding the time I spent on this dream of mine, and for your hard work in growing our firm.

Jan Miller, thanks for keeping me sane!

My blueberry babes Cheryl Hamilton, Nancy Roediger, Lisa Benedetti, Karen Parsons and you, too, Howard Hamilton, I appreciate your encouragement, thanks for listening, and thanks for my "Maine" experiences. Eddye Gallagher, Stacy and Eric Luecker, thanks for your input and encouragement. And Stacy (essexgraphix.com), thanks for taking my crazy ideas and designing such a great book cover and for all of the hand-holding you have given me during the process of producing this book. Tana Grubb, thanks for all of your great editing and for putting up with my stubbornness and accepting some of my crazy ideas. Erin Hamilton, thank you for proof-reading my work. Chuck Town, thanks for doing some of the research for this book.

My cutting edge study group, Fred Van Patten, Tony Lofaso, Curtis Shinn, Dave Tornetto, Steve Dahlquist, Jane Fontaine, Jim Izett and Jorge Vielledent. Thanks for challenging me and making me accountable to my goals. Also, Bill Green for your invaluable advice to us over the years.

My EWGA, NAWIC and BAC families, thanks to you, Fort Worth really is a small town, but in a good way.

My TCC board of directors, which include Joe and Faye Murphy, Sally Proffitt, Lanna Pruit, Virginia Freeman, Rudy Gonzales, Evette Brazille (and unofficially Ricardo Coronado) you all have really helped me be a better advisor to professors and employees of Tarrant County College.

My other board of advisors: Suzi Hill, (and Suzi, thanks for all of your encouragement to get involved in the community; and you probably don't know it, but when we first met, I had picked you as my one and only advisor at the time), Wayne Lawrence and Gail Warrior-Lawrence (you have both pushed me into "out of the box" thinking and challenged me and I appreciate that), John Brancato and Gina Puente-Brancato (thanks for your challenging me as well), JC Cole, Joanna Cloud, John Stone, Ed Turner, Bill and Sherri Rowell, Mike Sweet, Steve and Allyson Rahn, Isaac and Libby Manning (unofficially Frank and Dawn DeLeo). Thanks to all of you for giving me your honest feedback on how I can improve my practice and telling me when my ideas are a "little too crazy."

Ben Williams thanks for being my first real mentor and for your friendship. Andy Nelson, thanks for helping me feel welcome during my early days at AXA, for putting up with an immature 25 year-old, and for your friendship. Risa Philipose and Darrel Christian, thanks for being enthusiastic about my dream. Chris Noonan, Jeff Moore and Bob Auer, you are three people who believed in me before I believed in myself! Ken Comer, wherever you are, thanks for making me take that test seventeen years ago. Thanks to John Lefferts for his leadership, vision and desire for us to succeed.

Ricardo Coronado and Victor Puente, thanks for your encouragement, especially to write this section. It was very healing for me to write "my story." Author Kathy Kalina, thanks for your inspiration and for your book *"Mid Wife For Souls,"* which helped me get through one of the most difficult times in my life.

Pam Minick, thanks for your PR and marketing advice, your encouragement and enthusiasm.

The positive coaches in my life, Mark Frazier, you helped me have fun when I took golf and life too seriously! Ed Church, Jack Heinrichs, Sharon Quinn and Neil Crane, you all helped me have more discipline than I would have had without you. Garret Wheaton, you lead me by your great example, the way you lived your life, with your love for God, and the way you cared about your health.

Jack Lalane, you don't know me, but you were an inspiration to me. When as a kid, I would watch you on a black and white television, you would exercise with things as simple as a chair. You were before your time, and your desire to be fit and healthy made an impact on my life and created a desire in me to do so as well. Carol Burnett, besides great entertainment on many a Saturday night, you taught me how healing it is to laugh, and especially learning to laugh at myself.

And lastly, knowing that our business is a service business, and I decided to write a book about customer service, I knew my team better be able to back up what I had to say with great customer service for our firm.

So thanks to all of our clients, who challenge us to provide the best in customer service.

Wealth Strategy Advisors
~ *Giving you time for what matters most.*

Clockwise left to right: Allison Norman, James W. Taylor, Rebecca D. Turner, ChFC, and Brandon R. Howard

www.rebeccaturner.com
www.wealthstrategyadvisors.net

BIBLIOGRAPHY

Introduction—The Agreement
1. Kushner Harold S. *Living a Life That Matters*. Random House, Inc., New York, 2001.
2. Delagarza Dr. Thomas Michael, *The Agreement: Unlocking the Favor of God*. Falcon Publishing Company, Arlington TX, 2000 www.theagreementcenter.com

Why customer Advocates, Why Advocate Marketing?
1. Jones Laurie Beth *Jesus Life Coach*. Thomas Nelson, Inc.; Nashville, TN, 2004
2. West Scott and Anthony Mitch *Storyselling for Financial Advisors*. Dearborn Financial Publishing, Inc., 2000
3. Mackey Harvey B. *How to Swim With the Sharks Without Being Eaten Alive*. Random House, Inc., New York, 1988
4. Greenaway Kate *Mother Goose*. Reed Business Information, Inc., 1987
5. Buckingham Marcus *The One Thing you Need to Know*. A Division of Simon and Schuster, Inc., 2005
6. Blanchard Ken *Whale Done*. Blanchard Family Partnership and A Division of Simon and Schuster, Inc., 2002
7. Gerber Michael E. *The E-Myth Revisited*. Harper Collins Publisher, Inc., New York, 1995, 2001
8. Gladwell Malcolm *The Tipping Point: How Little Things Can Make a Big Difference*. Back Bay Books/Little, Brown and Company/ Time Warner Book Group, New York, 2000, 2002

Why Now?
1. Dent Harry S. *The Great Boom Ahead*. Library of Congress Cataloging-in-Publication Data, New York 1993

A Tire, a Roof, And a Package
1. Stanley Thomas J. and Danko William D. *The Millionaire Next Door*. Longstreet Press, Inc., 1996
2. Stanley Thomas J. *Millionaire Women Next Door*. Andrews McMeel Publishing, Kansas City Missouri, 2004

A Teacher, A Business Owner and A U.S Congresswoman
1. Gladwell Malcolm *Blink: The power of Thinking Without Thinking*. Little, Brown and Company/Time Warner Book Group, New York, 2005

About the Author
1. Thomas Frank P. *How to Write the Story of Your Life*. F+W Publications, Inc., 1989
2. Jensen Jamie *Road Trip USA*. Avalon Travel Publishing, Inc., 2002
3. Rim Sylvia *See Jane Win*. Three Rivers Press, New York, 1999
4. Dyer Wayne W. *The Power of Intention*. Hay House, Inc., Carlsbad CA, 2004
5. Kalina Kathy *Midwife for Souls*, Pauline Books and Media, 1995
6. McGee Robert S. *The Search for Significance*. Division of Thomas Nelson, Inc., 1998, 2003

ORDER FORM

To order additional copies
of this book, please visit the website
www.readtattoo.com

Call toll-free 1-888-232-4444
or fill out the order form and fax
1-250-383-6804
or mail this form and $19.95 + s/h to
Trafford Publishing
6E - 2333 Government Street
Victoria, BC, Canada V8T 4P4

(please print)

Name _____

Address _____

City _____ State _____ Zip _____

Phone _____

E-mail _____

Payment method

❑ Check   ❑ Money Order   ❑ Credit Card

❑ VISA   ❑ M/C   ❑ AMEX   ❑ Discover

Credit card number _____

Expiration _____

Name on card (if different from above) _____

Special instructions: